COUNSELLING FUNDAMENTALS IN THE WORKPLACE

For a complete list of Management Books 2000 titles,
visit our web-site on http://www.mb2000.com

COUNSELLING FUNDAMENTALS IN THE WORKPLACE

David McNorton

2000

First published in 2004 by Management Books 2000 Ltd
Forge House, Limes Road
Kemble, Cirencester
Gloucestershire, GL7 6AD, UK
Tel: 0044 (0) 1285 771441/2
Fax: 0044 (0) 1285 771055
E-mail: mb.2000@virgin.net
Web: www.mb2000.com

Printed and bound in Great Britain by Biddles of King's Lynn

British Library Cataloguing in Publication Data is available
ISBN 1-85252-446-4

Contents

Acknowledgments

Many people have contributed to the creation of this book and I'd like to thank all who have helped either directly or indirectly. First my family, Sooriya, Simon, Gareth, Luke and Joe for all the fun and companionship and Norma, Helen, Barry and Julie for their belief and support.

Professionally, I'd like to thank David Batman and Maxine Furnandiz for giving me the chance to practise and develop these ideas. A huge thanks to the whole Sensory Systems crowd who have been a cause of constant inspiration and challenge, especially Kate Watson, Carol Walker, Andy McWhirter, Shaun Moran, Chris Norris, Billy Haggarty, Billy Bonner, Colin and Sam Pritchard, Ruchirakatu, Karl Tooher, Richard and Roger Rees, Tim Ingerfield, Ian Robertson, Alan Unnuk and the many others who have been involved over the years.

I'd also like to thank Hugh Palmer for his constant encouragement and light relief.

Finally a very special thanks to two people who above all have made this book possible. To my late father Bill McNorton who inadvertently started me out in this adventure many years ago, and John McWhirter, a great friend and an inspirational teacher.

1

An Introduction To Counselling

In the early 1990s, I was asked to design and facilitate an introductory course in counselling for the Occupational Health nurses of a large manufacturing company. The idea was that these nurses would be trained to a level that would allow them to carry out basic supportive counselling and assessment for employees of the company. They would do this under professional supervision and would also have professional counsellors to refer on to, should they find themselves out of their depth. This meant that the course would also need to provide the participants with some counselling needs assessment skills.

The course ran on an annual basis for over seven years and was generally considered to be a great success, providing participants with key fundamental skills. Of course, the structure and contents of the course evolved during that time as our understanding of what was needed changed.

This book is based almost exclusively on that course and I hope that it allows me to share with you some of what I have learned about counselling in the workplace and the learning of fundamental counselling skills.

The book is aimed at anyone with an interest in counselling or who thinks that some basic counselling skills would help in their day-to-day work. That probably applies to most people working in large organisations today, especially if they have some responsibility towards the welfare of other employees.

During my time working in industry, I have worked alongside many very capable and skilled managers who experienced difficulty when faced with more complex personnel or staff relationship difficulties. Many complained that they simply weren't trained or prepared to deal with more emotional, human type problems. Some managed well relying on their natural social skills whilst others struggled, perhaps feeling that the 'soft' side of management was not really their forte. I very quickly came to realise that most would benefit from basic training in counselling. If you feel that there have been times when you have been a little out of your depth when dealing with staff problems, or maybe even that you could have done with a little more training to give you the confidence to deal with them adequately, then you can benefit from this book.

Whether we like it or not, staff problems are becoming increasingly the responsibility of organisation managers. Whereas once upon it time, it may have been enough to tell staff to leave their problems at home, today's manager has to take a more active interest in the welfare of his or her workforce. In part, this is because in reality the problems don't get left at home and do affect work performance – sometimes quite catastrophically – and this in turn affects the department's and company's performance. A manager is responsible for this and so being able to support and help staff through difficult times is a crucial skill.

In 1990, the Health & Safety Executive published figures which showed that 40,000,000 working days a year were lost through stress and stress-related illness in this country alone. That was over ten years ago and the trend is on the up – stress has reached epidemic proportions. Increasingly, companies and organisations are being held either partially or wholly responsible for this stress and there have already been some significant legal actions taken against organisations by staff suffering though stress. By developing useful counselling skills, a modern manager can not only help to reduce workplace stress but also show the world that he or she is taking positive action to tackle workplace stress.

Counselling is not the only way in which staff can be helped through their personal difficulties but it does have a well-proven track record over the past forty years or so and is probably most people's first choice of approach when seeking help. Certainly the last twenty years has seen a boom in counselling services with 2002 seeing the

British Association of Counselling & Psychotherapy membership exceeding 20,000. Despite criticism from some areas of the news and media, counselling is now widely recognised as an effective and essential part of modern health care.

By now, you will, I hope, realise that the counselling in the workplace we are discussing here is about using counselling to help people through difficulties. This is not to be confused with the way the term counselling is sometimes used by managers and organisations as a polite way of describing a dressing down given to some unfortunate employee who is not performing well. At no time, will I discuss counselling as part of any disciplinary procedure.

'Counsellor' and 'client'

Throughout the book, I shall use the terms counsellor and client when referring to the two people involved in the counselling situation. I will describe many types of counselling situations, so don't be put off if these terms seems a little grandiose in describing the kind of counselling situation you might find yourself in. It is simply for convenience that I use these terms.

The book is split into two sections. Section one deals with basic counselling theory and skills including such things as the counselling attitude, building rapport, counselling psychology, questioning and information gathering. Section two is more concerned with the practical applications of counselling.

I have tried to keep exercises to a minimum mainly because most of the training exercises we use in counselling training involve at least two people and for that reason might be difficult for you, the reader, to practice. For some aspects of counselling skills training, there is however simply no replacement for good experiential exercises so I urge you to complete each of these to the best of your ability. They are invaluable learning tools and, unless you do experience them, it is unlikely that you will be in a position to practice even supportive counselling with any degree of competence.

Of course, a book of this kind can never really replace a more thorough training and it is certainly not intended to turn you into a counsellor overnight. Full time professional counsellors, like any other profession, have to study hard over several years training before they are considered competent to practice. What I hope it does provide you with is some fundamental skills-based training in the basic communication techniques of counselling as well as an understanding and appreciation of some of the major issues involved in counselling in the workplace.

Despite this, there remain many, ill-informed members of the public who still believe that all there is to counselling is the application of a little common sense. If only this were indeed the case, we would have far less emotional trauma, anxiety, depression and stress than we do. In fact, counselling, in its modern form, is a highly skilled activity requiring high levels of concentration, awareness and understanding. It is not something that can be learned overnight and neither is it something to be 'dabbled in'. If you are serious about developing skills as a counsellor, then this book should really just be the beginning.

I have included many example transcripts of client sessions, throughout the book. In the absence of being able to provide live experience as we might during a training course, these offer tangible and hopefully illuminating insights into the more theoretical aspects of counselling. In the second section, lengthier transcripts are included with some level of explanation as examples of three different levels of counselling.

Modern counselling dates back to the 1950s. Before this, people relied on a mixture of friends, family, family doctors and priests to provide them with support in times of trouble. But, as the twentieth century progressed, the pace of life picked up considerably with an explosion of cultural changes bringing ever-greater complexity to life. These changes also saw the slow disintegration of the extended family as the social norm and with this went the support such a unit provided. As opportunities increased in education, business and social life, we in the west enjoyed greater freedoms than any of our predecessors. And with all of these freedoms came the flip side; isolation, loneliness, alienation, fear, anger, anxiety and stress only now there is often no one to turn to with the time, understanding and skills to help. Counselling emerged in the 1950s as one way of filling this void.

Karl Rogers

In its modern context, the word counselling was first coined by US psychologist Karl Rogers, the developer of the first approach to modern counselling, the 'Client Centred' approach. At that time there were strict laws in the US governing who could and couldn't help others in a professional capacity. Psychotherapy was already an accepted discipline but could only be practiced by doctors of medicine and so, despite his approach having many similarities to some schools of psychotherapy, Rogers called his approach counselling and began to teach this to others, including social workers and teachers – professionals who were not medically qualified.

Through his writings and through his direct teachings in seminars and workshops, Rogers' ideas and theories on counselling quickly became the standard for the new and burgeoning profession of counselling.

Since the 1950s, others have both added to and deviated from Rogers' original ideas although most forms of counselling still hold true to the central tenant of Rogerian counselling; that it be client centred. In counselling, it is the client that is considered the expert in his or her own life, problems, difficulties and solutions. The role of the counsellor is to facilitate change and problem resolution but it is not the role of the counsellor to decide on what that change should be or to resolve problems for the client.

This very non-prescriptive approach to helping people deal with the difficulties in life is often at odds with what most lay-people might do instinctively to help a friend or loved one. The giving and taking of advice is commonplace within our culture but in counselling this is normally frowned upon. Why? Well, Rogers and others since him, argued that for a healthy and well-organised change to take place, the solution should begin and end with the client so that he or she takes full ownership of the problem and its resolution. This is empowering in that clients create their own solutions. It is also more likely to be fully congruent, that is in keeping with the client's make up, experience and general outlook on life. But even more than this, it is the client and not the problem that should be the central concern for the Rogerian counsellor. If the client works through the process of counselling, becoming more aware and more in tune with his- or herself then, the advocates of Rogerian counselling argue, the problems resolve themselves or at the very least the client is now better able to resolve them without the need of outside advice.

One of the drawbacks of this approach is that, because the counsellor's role is simply to facilitate resolution, that resolution can be a long time coming and it is not at all unusual for client-centred counselling to go on for many, many sessions with the counsellor offering encouragement and support as the client struggles to find answers. For this reason, other methods of counselling have developed that offer slightly more in the way of a structure or even procedure for guiding the client through a process of problem resolution more efficiently. Gerard Egan, for example, in his seminal book *'The Skilled Helper'* outlines a tightly structured approach to counselling that is becoming increasingly popular.

Systemic counselling

The ideas and principles in this book are based almost exclusively on a relatively new approach called 'Systemic Counselling', which differs from the more traditional approaches to counselling in that it does not begin from the basic distinction of 'client centred' or 'problem centred'. Instead it is both client and problem centred. It is not the counsellor that comes up with solutions, neither is it the client – it is rather both, working together as a team or 'system' that arrive at solutions with each bringing to the situation their own particular skills and understanding. Clients obviously know the circumstances that have led to their problems or difficulties better than anyone, in this and in their own life they are the true experts. The counsellors bring a very different expertise. Systemic counsellors' expertise lies in a grasp of the processes of human understanding, communication and change. They are skilled at helping clients gather together and organise the relevant information and personal resources and in helping the clients identify, plan and implement meaningful resolutions. For this reason alone, systemic counselling offers perhaps the most effective, efficient and elegant approach to counselling currently available and is therefore an excellent choice for the busy workplace.

Indeed, in the ten years that I have provided a counselling service to organisations and industry, it is rare for the total number of client sessions to exceed six, hour-long sessions. That is not to say that every client problem is resolved following this but, in the cases where no resolution is found or the client is not helped in some way, both the counsellor and client will typically know this at the end of the six sessions and have a good understanding of what should come next.

There are of course occasions when counselling continues for considerably longer than this but these are usually more complex cases that would in any case have required some kind of intervention, quite possibly medical, sooner or later.

The efficiency of systemic counselling obviously makes it popular in large and busy organisations, but that is not all. The skills and understandings developed through training in systemic counselling have far more long-reaching benefits because many are universal life skills that can be used and applied in other aspects of the counsellor's working and home life. Systemic counselling skills are not just a set of skills that are brought out when in the counselling situation. Many of the models for problem resolution for example have everyday applications in the counselling student's life.

I want to talk briefly about the origins and development of Systemic Counselling. I feel that this helps provide some historical context. Its development is almost exclusively the work of Scottish trainer and therapist John McWhirter, whose own interest in human change and therapy began in the early 1980s. McWhirter started out by studying Gestalt therapy but soon became interested in the exciting new discipline of Neuro-Linguistic Programming (NLP). McWhirter was a very capable student and soon became a trainer in NLP, working closely for several years with NLP founder Richard Bandler. NLP was itself an interesting fusion of ideas on communication and change that had been created by mathematics student Richard Bandler and Professor of Linguistics John Grinder in California in the early 1970s. NLP drew upon the work of linguist Noam Chomsky, the ideas and theories of systems and cybernetics of Gregory Bateson, the psychology of Fritz Perls and the general semantics movement created by Korzybski. There were other influences but these formed the core.

McWhirter took the basic ideas of NLP and began to develop a more total and holistic approach to counselling and therapy. Over several years he built, tested and consolidated these ideas. In 1993, the first Diploma in Systemic Counselling was introduced and since then many students have qualified as systemic counsellors.

When designing the six-day introductory course it was a relatively easy task to select those aspects of systemic counselling to include and all of these I have replicated in this book so that hopefully you will read this and feel a sense that you are well equipped to begin your adventure into counselling.

The systemic counselling method

I want to begin with a general framework or method that provides an overview of the systemic counselling approach. As you progress in your understanding of systemic counselling, this method will provide a reference point and help organise your learning.

We can break down a typical counselling intervention into several key stages, which we shall call the Systemic Counselling Method. Following each of these stages in a methodical fashion helps ensure a successful counselling intervention. Figure 1 opposite details these stages and each will be covered in more depth in subsequent chapters.

- The client-counsellor relationship needs to be soundly built upon trust and mutual respect. The counsellor taking active steps to develop rapport achieves this but rapport alone is clearly not enough.

- The first purpose of developing this mutual trust is in order for the counsellor to begin gathering information about the client and the client's unique situation. The counsellor will be questioning and exploring in some depth and this can sometimes be quite challenging for the client. Without rapport, the client may well find the challenge too much and chose not to share important information with the counsellor.

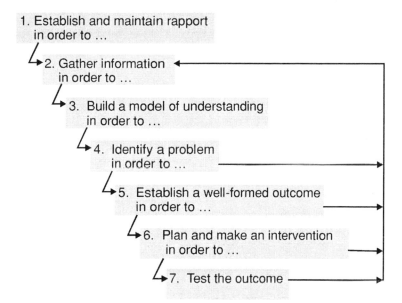

Figure 1

- As the counsellor gathers information, an understanding emerges which is shared between counsellor and client. In systemic counselling, we refer to this as a 'model' of understanding. This reminds us that no matter how thorough our information gathering, we can never know every thing there is to know about the client and the situation. What we have is a model and that will always be an impoverished version of 'the truth'.

- In building an understanding, we will begin to isolate the client's problem. At this stage it is worth considering that not every client that comes for counselling has a problem as such. As you will see later, some clients simply require support through a difficult or challenging situation and in its strictest sense it would be wrong to describe them as having a problem.

● Assuming however that we are able to identify a problem, the next stage is to arrive at a well-formed outcome. It is not enough to know what it is the client is trying to overcome. Our task is to help clients identify clearly where they want to get to – their outcome for counselling.

● With an outcome in place, we are able, together with the client, to design and implement some kind of intervention or interventions that will help the client achieve the outcome.

● Finally, and crucially, we need to test our work. Has the client truly achieved the desired outcome and, if not, what more might we need to do to help.

Laid out in this way, it would be easy to fall into the trap of thinking that this process is linear and that each stage always falls neatly from the last. In practice, it is common to find oneself circling around these in a more complex fashion and the arrows in the diagram indicate this. For example we might arrive at an understanding of a problem and set about trying to arrive at a well-formed outcome. Through the process of doing this we might find that we never really had a useful understanding of the problem in the first place and so need to go back and gather more information in order to get a better handle on things.

This method is intended as a guide only and is not intended to be used as a procedure that has to be slavishly followed. At various times, you will need to spend more or less time at different stages of the process depending on the unique circumstances of each counselling session. For example, with some clients, rapport will be easy to achieve, requiring very little effort on your part whilst with others, you may need to spend considerably more time building this basic trust.

Levels of counselling

I have already mentioned that not every client that we see for counselling has a problem and this might sound a little contrary on first reading – after all why would anyone require counselling if they don't have a problem to start with?

I am going to distinguish three levels of counselling and one of the central purposes of this book is to detail what these differences are and their implications on exactly what is required from the counsellor. To practice safely as a counsellor, it is vital that we work safely within our own level of competence and, understanding these different counselling needs helps ensure this.

Level 1: Supportive counselling

The Client is experiencing distressing but normal life events:

- redundancy
- bereavement
- victim of crime
- life threatening illness
- divorce or separation.

The counsellor offers support and friendship.
The goals of counselling are:
1. acceptance
2. the prevention of problem development.

Level 2: Problem-solving counselling

The client is experiencing practical problems requiring solutions:

- decision making
- financial difficulties
- time management
- planning and organisation.

The counsellor helps the client explore possible solutions.
The goals of counselling are:
1. to find an appropriate solution
2. to ensure that the solution is ecological for the client and those around them.

Level 3: Therapeutic counselling (psychotherapy)

The client is experiencing problems with the difficulties of life:

- depression
- anxiety
- low self-esteem
- problems establishing and maintaining relationships
- addiction
- stress.

The counsellor remodels the client's model and modelling of the world. The goals of counselling are:

to help the client think, feel and behave more usefully – this means effective as well as affective change.

In the second part of this book each of these levels will be dealt with in its own chapter where more concrete examples of each will be provided.

Reading this book and practicing the exercises within should provide you with the basic skills and understanding to begin providing some supportive counselling together with the ability to more accurately assess the counselling needs of a client, should you need to refer to a more experienced counsellor. We look at problem-solving counselling and some tools are provided to help you make a start in this slightly more complex level of counselling. Therapeutic counselling is included to provide you with some insight into what is involved but it is not intended that you would be in a position to conduct this level of counselling on the basis of reading this book.

This book will not prepare you for the higher levels of counselling or psychotherapy but, with the skills you can develop through careful reading and following of the exercises, you should be well equipped to carry out supportive counselling and to assess when higher levels of counselling are required.

2

The Counselling Attitude

There is a popular misconception that counsellors are somehow a unique breed of person with unusual qualities of compassion, sympathy and sensitivity. The stereotypical counsellor has an abundance of patience and an ability to take on and solve all the world's ills. Many student counsellors question whether they are really made of the 'right stuff' to cut it as a counsellor.

Whilst it is true that many counsellors, through a combination of past experience and inherent characteristics, are particularly good at developing interpersonal relationships, counselling like any other occupation incorporates a wide diversity of personality types. For example, it is not necessarily the case that a counsellor needs to be particularly sensitive or sympathetic, although many are. There are very many skilled and competent counsellors who do not fit the stereotypical profile of a counsellor and yet they still do very effective work.

What we are dealing with here is a very important aspect of counselling skills development that we shall call the COUNSELLING ATTITUDE and the good news is that a healthy and useful counselling attitude can be learned and developed.

Developing the counselling attitude is really the starting point in becoming more skilled in counselling. Many of my counselling students are initially apprehensive about the thought of counselling people with problems and the development of the right attitude certainly helps to overcome these fears. There are two themes to these fears – the first is the fear that they might become overwhelmed by the client's problems. Students will often ask how I, as a full time counsellor, switch off after spending a day listening to other people's problems almost as if these problems were somehow contagious. The second is the fear that they will not know what to say or what to do to help the client. There is a tendency amongst new counselling students to dive in with solutions almost before the client has had a chance to explain what their problem or difficulty is. The pressure to come up with answers is self-created, and born of the fear that they might not know what to say. One of the most important lessons to learn when you begin to counsel others is not to rush in, and it is best you learn this lesson quickly. Just remember that angels fear.

Fortunately both of these fears can be overcome by the development of a useful counselling attitude. Not only that but the development of the counselling attitude helps ensure that your counselling is safe, thorough and professional.

The counselling attitude is a combination of three components or aspects. These are:

1. **Curiosity** – having a real and genuine interest in the client; a willingness to want to find out all you can about the client and his or her story.

2. **Outcome Focused** – the ability and desire to remain focussed on the general outcome of counselling; to help the client overcome the problem.

3. **Rapport** – understanding the importance and value of establishing and maintaining rapport and trust with the client.

To develop the counselling attitude, we need to place equal emphasis on each of these and learn how we can develop and access these in the counselling situation. We have already mentioned rapport in chapter one and it is of such importance that we shall be devoting a whole chapter to it later in the book. For now, we shall concentrate of the first two, **curiosity** and being **outcome focused**.

We can think of these as being particular frames of mind or states and you can probably recall times when you have been particularly curious about something, a hobby or interest or particular issue in your life. Equally you can probably think of times when you have been particularly focused on a specific outcome – maybe when you've had a work deadline to achieve for example. As an exercise it will be worth taking a little time out to recall just what these experiences were like.

Firstly take a sheet of notepaper and list a few occasions from your past when you have felt particularly curious. Don't worry about the context, these could be work related or connected to a particular hobby or interest. The only thing they need to have in common is that you found them particularly interesting; that you wanted to find out all you could about what was going on. The state of curiosity is one that usually comes very easily to us; it is one of the qualities that defines what it is to be human.

Now, with your list in hand step back into each of these memories. The more vividly you can reconnect with them, the more easily you will be able to re-access that state of curiosity, so give yourself time and focus on just exactly how it felt to be that curious. In particular, connect with the specific feelings they have in common irrespective of the content or context. This is a state of pure curiosity.

Next imagine that you are sitting down to listen to your first counselling client and take those feelings of curiosity with you. This is a technique very similar to that used by method actors. In method acting, if an actor's character needs to express a particular emotion, the actor will often recall times when they have experienced that emotion in their own lives and take that into the acting situation. It isn't really acting at all because at the time they really are experiencing the emotion, which is one of the reasons why method acting is such a convincing form of acting.

One of the benefits of using this approach with the state of curiosity is that it becomes self re-enforcing. The human mind tends to adapt quickly and the importance of an activity increases the more time we spend on it. The more curious you are, the more curious you become.

If you have the opportunity, it is well worth spending some time practicing this with a friend or colleague. Sit down with them and simply chat about them or something they have experienced. Be very curious – all that should be on your mind is to find out as much as you can about them. At first this may seem a little false or unnatural but you will be surprised at how quickly it becomes second nature.

Being curious when counselling is clearly important. If we are not at least in part curious, we will never learn anything about our clients or why they are seeing us, and therefore be unable to offer any help. But, there are two other more subtle benefits that emerge from the counsellor's curiosity. The first is that the counsellor's curiosity validates the client's experience. Often clients come to us confused and unsure about some aspect of their lives or themselves. Being curious and exploring the clients' experience lets the clients know that we value their understanding that we consider their experience to be important – why else would be spending time exploring it with them?

> A young clerical worker came for counselling, complaining of feeling unwanted by his manager. For a number of months, he had been largely ignored and on the rare occasions that he did have contact received nothing but negative feedback from the manager. Now the client knew that he felt bad but wasn't sure whether this was due to his treatment or something else. Was he over-reacting? Perhaps it was just the way things were and it was his problem. By exploring his feelings at length and spending time listening to him describe his experiences, the counsellor was able to convey the idea that the young man's experience was considered important; that it was perfectly valid for him to feel this way.

The second benefit is that our curiosity becomes contagious. Clients will often try to avoid dwelling on or thinking about their problems because they are unpleasant. They may try to pretend that all is well when clearly it is not. By being curious and showing that we are willing to question and explore the most difficult and unpleasant experiences, we are helping them to learn that they can do the same. We are teaching the clients a pattern of curiosity, a pattern that helps them face their difficulties and ultimately learn how they might be overcome.

Being curious about clients and their stories in this way is not so very different from the kind of attitude we might often label as 'nosey'. Indeed I often joke with students that one of the reasons I enjoy counselling so much is that heart I'm just a nosey so and so. But, of course, if curiosity was all there was to the counselling attitude, then this label would be fully appropriate. If we were simply curious and nothing more, then our client sessions would wander all over the place with no real sense of direction or purpose – which is why the second component of the counselling attitude, being **outcome focused**, is so important.

Much as you did with the attitude of curiosity, take a little time out and recall times from your past when you have felt particularly outcome focused. Again, identifying times from different contexts will be useful. Note these down on a sheet of notepaper. And, once more, step back into each of these experiences recalling just how it felt to be that focused on a particular outcome. As you do this, remind yourself that it is not the specific outcome that is important but rather that achieving outcomes of any sort is what is important. Don't become to entangled with the specific content of each memory. It should be as if you are distilling the very essence of what it is to be outcome focused from these memories.

Once more, if you have the opportunity, sit down with a friend or colleague and talk about something that is of interest to them. Retain the sense of curiosity you developed earlier but now layer in the need to focus on an outcome. In this case, the outcome could be something like finding out all you can about the colleague's specific experience but nothing more. If the conversation starts to digress, being outcome focused should help you draw it back to your specific outcome of finding out all you can.

Unlike the first experience of simply being curious, what you should find is that, once an outcome is focused on, the conversation becomes much more targeted. Your questions are no longer asked for curiosity's sake alone but because you have more specific information you wish to uncover. Of course, the problem with this is that your friend is likely to have an experience somewhat akin to being interrogated as your curiosity fires off question after question and your need to achieve an outcome directs the course the conversation takes. Notice how they respond. Often you will see them becoming increasingly defensive and reluctant to talk. Hopefully you picked a good friend or at the very least someone who understands that you are exploring in order to develop counselling skills.

By adding the third component of the counselling attitude, rapport and the need to maintain rapport, our exploration becomes more cautious and less forceful. We start to attend to how the client is responding and place the major emphasis on maintaining rapport and so avoid their having the experience of being interrogated by our questioning. This means that rapport must override all other considerations. Without rapport, we cannot influence and without the ability to influence we will not be able to counsel. Equally being outcome-focused overrides being curious. As counsellors, we should avoid being curious for curiosity's sake alone but rather always try to ensure that our curiosity is tempered by the need to remain focused on the outcome of counselling.

So, we can create a nested hierarchy for our three components of the counselling attitude.

- Overall, we need to maintain **rapport**.
- Within that, we should strive to do all we can to **achieve the outcome** of our counselling ...
- ... and within that we should be just as **curious** as we can about the client and their experience.

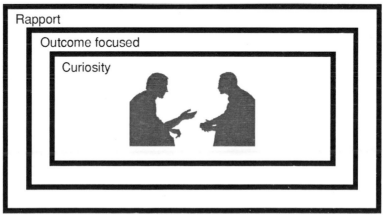

Figure 2

Rather than thinking of these three as being absolute states that we are either in or not in, it is more useful to conceptualise them as dynamic directions. The reason for this is that they become easier to access and 'get into'. Rather than worrying about whether we are curious or not, we can think instead about just how curious we are at any one time. This helps enormously because there will often be times when you feel tired or lacking in resources or simply when you are preoccupied with other issues and yet find yourself having to put aside time to counsel a member of staff. You remind yourself that you need to be curious, that you need to be focused on outcome and so on, but somehow because of everything else that is going on you just can't re-access those states, at least not in the same way and with the same quality as when you did the above exercises. But in reality, it is an over-simplification to think of these states in such black and white terms. Instead, thinking of them as analogues means that you can at least place yourself somewhere along the path to becoming more curious or becoming more outcome focused. It gives a starting point and a direction.

3

The Nature of Experience

Counselling is mostly concerned with understanding. That is, the counsellor's understanding of the client but, more importantly the client's own understanding of self. Through the process of counselling, counsellors aims to enrich and change clients' understanding of themselves and their world.

Human understanding begins with the five senses, these are visual, auditory, kinaesthetic (including tactile), olfactory and gustatory and it is only through these five senses that we can ever know anything at all. The first three are of most importance in human understanding with the olfactory (smell) and gustatory (taste) senses playing only a minor role.

Humans never know the world in a direct objective sense but rather build a subjective understanding through the senses. The senses are our interface with the outside world. In systemic counselling we call this process **Modelling** and the understanding that is constructed by the individual is called their **Model**.

The senses work by reacting to stimuli. Within each sense, there are specialist cells or arrays of cells that are capable of reacting to a particular type of stimulus. In the case of the visual sense, the eyes contain specialist cells within the retina that react to a range of light frequencies. When one cell reacts but another doesn't, a difference is detected and it is the noticing of this difference or the making of a distinction that is the basis of all sensory input. The senses notice and respond to difference and in order to do this they are constantly being re-stimulated. The eyes, if looked at closely, can be seen to be constantly vibrating in tiny movements. This movement is known as micro-nystagmus and its purpose is to re-stimulate the light sensitive cells of the retina. If they are not re-stimulated, they simply shut down and no difference can be detected. In Arctic and Antarctic conditions, people often experience a temporary inability to see – known as snow blindness. This occurs if the person spends too long looking out on the unchanging view of a snowscape. There is no news of a difference despite the eyes' micro-movements; everything is a uniform white and eventually the cells in the retina close down. Ultimately, all of understanding begins with and is built upon the senses' ability to notice a difference.

There is a popular cliché in the world of constructivist psychology that 'the map is not the territory'. The idea behind this is straightforward. A map should never contain all the information of the territory it maps. If it did so then it would be so large and so detailed that it would be of no practical use, it would be identical to the territory. When we draw maps, we include only as much information as we think will be needed by the user of the map. We simplify by selecting to include some parts of the territory and, by default, leaving other parts out. We can think of a human model of understanding like a map. In building an understanding of a situation, we select only those details that we consider important or relevant. The senses respond only to the important differences. From there on, cognitive processes construct an understanding, and that construction, that model, is always and necessarily a simplification and interpretation of the events of the outside world.

For many years, psychologists believed that information processing from the senses was *bottom up*. What this means is that what finally impinges on our awareness as a representation of the outside world is determined purely by the primary sensory stimulus. In other words, the information passes only one way and that is up from the senses to the brain and to our awareness. We now know that this is not the case, that in fact even at the very early stages of the process, our sensing is being organised by other cognitive processes in what is know as *top down* processing. The following optical illusion helps demonstrate the significance of top down processing.

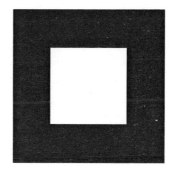

Figure 3

Which of the two squares in the centre of the larger squares appears bigger? Some people think that the left hand black box looks bigger but for most it is the right hand white box that appears bigger. Of course, objectively they are the same size.

When we examine how this illusion works, some very interesting facts about human sensing are revealed. All of our senses have the ability to focus on one specific stimulus from within a larger collection of multiple stimuli. If you look around you now, your attention will naturally focus on certain objects. These objects become the foreground or centre of attention and everything else falls into the background. This process of foregrounding is necessary in order that we can focus on specific things and, in evolutionary terms, aids our survival because it means we can focus on specific threats or rewards. In our natural environment, the environment where the senses evolved, foreground objects were likely to have been lighter and background objects darker. When we look at the above illusion, the smaller white box on the right is automatically and unconsciously assumed to be foreground and therefore literally brought forward in our vision. The black box on the left is assumed to be background and therefore pushed back. Because it is subjectively closer, the white box is seen as bigger, the black box, subjectively further away as smaller.

Another interesting example is the colour black on older TV sets. If you look at an older TV screen (older being one with a dull grey screen), when the TV is off, the screen is a dull grey colour. When the TV is on and a black object is shown, the black object appears much darker than the grey of the off-screen, even though black is produced by turning off all cathode ray bombardment of that part of the screen. In other words, turning that part of the screen off produces black. So, how can a black object appear darker when the screen is in exactly the same state? Partly this can be explained by the idea that we always view objects in relation to other objects and a larger background, so that the colour of an object is seen as relative to other surrounding colours.

So if we consider these two examples, apart from the fact that we can't trust our senses to inform us in any objective way, what does this tell us about human understanding?

It tells us that human understanding can never be 'true' understanding in an objective sense so, instead, it is more accurate to think of understanding as more or less useful. Our models of understanding, like the maps we talked about earlier, need not be accurate and direct representations – they merely need to serve a purpose. Once we let go of the idea of truth in understanding, it becomes easier to see how understanding can be richer or poorer, useful or less useful and that both our and our clients' understanding of their experience can be changed and can potentially become more useful. When we sit down with a client, it is important to remind ourselves that our role is not to change the world of the client but rather to work with and change the client's understanding of that world. Here's another, perhaps more relevant, example of the fickle nature of human understanding.

In 1979, experimental psychologist Dr Elizabeth Loftus reported on a remarkable experiment, which showed just how unreliable eyewitness testimonies could be. Experimental subjects were each shown a short film of a car accident. They were then questioned by the experimenters on what they had seen. However, the experimenters made subtle changes to the questions they asked in order to see how these influenced the subject's answers. For example some subjects were asked the question 'How fast was the yellow car going when it *collided with* the red car?' while others were asked the question 'How fast was the yellow car going when it *smashed into* the red car?' There was a significant difference in the answers with subjects answering the second question reporting the car going faster than those answering the first question. The change in the question had influenced the subjects' recall of the incident.

Now I hope the relevance of this to counselling can be readily seen. Much of what we do as counsellors is questioning in order to explore but, when we see just how easily our questions can influence the understanding of the client, then we need to take great care over how we question. Of course this is double-edged because, once we are aware of this, we can use our questioning creatively to help the client build a more useful understanding of his or her experience.

Take the following example.

A young and newly appointed receptionist was having problems adjusting to her new work environment. She was the only woman working in an office of men, most of whom had been working for the company for many years. The receptionist felt intimidated by her fellow workers and this was making her nervous and affecting her work performance. The following brief dialogue took place on her first visit to a counsellor.

Receptionist: You should see what it's like, they're always laughing and joking and most of the time I don't understand their jokes. It's awful. I just feel so out of place.

Counsellor: And, since you've been there, I guess you get on with some of them better than others. Which of them do you get on best with?

Receptionist: (Smiling) Oh, that's easy. Mark. He's actually quite sweet once you get to know him.

Counsellor: So what makes Mark easier to get on with than some of the others?

Receptionist: Well, there are a couple of them really. Mark and Gavin. They asked me out for a drink the other night but some of the others were going as well, so I decided not to. Do you think I should have gone?

Counsellor: I don't really know. It would have been a chance to get to know Mark and Gavin better I suppose, in a different sort of environment. But, since you're friends with them, maybe you could suggest just the three of you going out sometime.

Over the course of this brief dialogue, the counsellor uses certain presupposed words in his questioning that impact upon the receptionist's understanding. He separates out the group of men so that rather than seeing them as the whole intimidating group, she now sees potential allies within the group. This is reinforced by his use of the words 'friends' when referring to them in a later question. As it turned out, the receptionist became very good friends with the two men she mentioned and was soon feeling considerably more comfortable at work.

The process of creating a model of understanding is sometimes referred to as the process of *abstraction*. This is because the building of any model or map requires for efficiency's sake that information be stored in a simplified form. We experience the world through our senses but as we have seen, before the experience begins to register on our awareness, some abstraction has already taken place. The sensory-based representation we experience subjectively is never the complete picture.

But, humans also possess an amazing tool that as far as we know is not available to any other species of life – language. It is through the use of language that we are able to most effectively abstract meaning from sensory experience and then reason on the basis of that abstraction. Once we are able to use language to label objects and processes, then we can enrich our model of understanding and, using the power of reasoning, predict likely outcomes of our actions in the world.

If we take the word 'friend' as an example. Without ever having to think about each and every friend we have we are able to use this word or label to reason about all sorts of aspects of friendship. We could think about how we might expect our friends to behave towards us and how that might be different from the way non-friends behave. We can select who belongs to the group we call friends and who does not. We can even redefine our understanding of the word 'friends' if people we

A schematic representation of the abstracting process

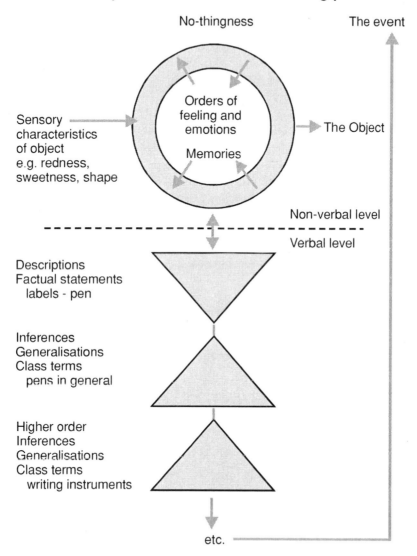

Taken from Weinberg's 'Levels of Knowing and Existence'

Figure 4

consider friends behave differently than expected. Words and language allow us to distil meaning from the world in a remarkably efficient way.

Within language, there are words that are more or less abstract. Some, more sensory-based, descriptive words are clearly less abstract and therefore closer to the original sensory experience they are based on, while other less descriptive words are much more abstract. The structure and importance of this abstracting process was highlighted by Alfred Korzybski in his pioneering work *'Science and Sanity'* which sparked the establishment of a new school of thinking known as General Semantics. General Semantics is, as the name suggests, concerned with meaning and its construction, therefore making it a constructivist approach to human psychology.

We have used the word model to describe the understanding we each have of the world in which we live. During the 1970s, the pioneers of NLP modelled the structure of this understanding. They were interested in the structure of subjective models or the representation of subjective experience.

Through this work, it was discovered that our subjective experience is built upon the primary senses and the use of language; that is to say that we represent the world to ourselves as a series of images, movies, sounds, feelings, words etc. These distinctions became known as the representational systems and it was found that a person's experience could be understood by tracking through sequences of these representational systems. For example, suppose we were to ask two people to recall a time when they had some difficulty making a decision. Person one subjectively represents the memory as a series of pictures accompanied by some relatively strong negative feelings. However, person two has no subjective images in the recall of the experience but rather relives it by running an internal commentary of what occurred accompanied by an overall negative feeling of discomfort. Person two largely relies on language to recall the events.

Although each person's subjective recall is markedly different in both content and form, what is universal is that each must necessarily make use of representational systems to recall the experience.

The representational systems are based on the five senses although taste and smell are less commonly used to represent our experiences. And, NLP has developed a shorthand notation for recording sequences of these representations.

The Representational Systems

Representational System	Notation
Visual	V
Auditory (Analogues sounds)	A
Kinaesthetic	K
Olfactory	O
Gustatory	G
Auditory (Digital or Language)	Ad

So, if we were to notate the subjective experiences of the two examples from above we might get something like:

Person 1   V , -V, K-, V, K-, V, V, K-
Person 2.   Ad, K-

As the developers of NLP explored this further, they discovered that quite often sequences repeated themselves and they realised that individuals learned and developed their own unique sequences for representing or processing certain cognitive skills. These sequences or strategies could be both useful and limiting and discovering more about an individual's strategies became a very useful tool for counsellors and therapists in helping understand and bring about change for their clients. For example a client might report that he has problems with starting new projects; that he keeps putting things off. The counsellor can help the client identify the particular representational sequence or strategy for this by exploring various examples and noticing the common elements within the representational sequence. They might, for instance, discover that whenever the client thinks about a new project, he forms a series of internal images of the project at various projected stages of completion. At the end of the sequence, he may get a large and very positive feeling of a 'job well done' even though in reality he has not even begun the project. This positive feeling may well be enough to sustain him so that he doesn't ever feel a need to actually complete the project.

Understanding a client's strategy in this way is just the first stage in helping him or her develop a new and more useful strategy. To find out more about NLP representational systems and strategies, I suggest the excellent book *'The Structure of Magic II'*. This was one of the first, and in my opinion best, books on NLP from the 1970s.

Later, in the early 1980s, Richard Bandler introduced further distinctions to subjective representations that he called **submodalities**. It is said that Bandler came up with this distinction after asking himself just how it was that one representation in a sequence or strategy led to the next. What determines the order and elements of a sequence? To answer this, he looked further into the structure and make-up of specific sensory representations and discovered that here too, there was a universality that could be both understood and utilised.

The notion on submodalities is best understood through example. Take an internal representation from the visual system – for example, recall and bring to mind a particular holiday experience that you enjoyed. Picture that memory in your mind's eye. Now, as you look at that image, how clear is it? How **bright** is the image? Is it particularly **colourful** or, is it more like a **black and white** image? Do you see the image as if it was **far** off in front of you or does it look **close**? Is there **movement** in the image or is it like a **still** snapshot? Do you **see** yourself in the image, like seeing yourself in a photo or video (**dissociated**) or, is it as if you were there again, seeing through your eyes and reliving the experience as it was (**associated**)?

Each of these questions highlights a distinction in how a representation can be structured irrespective of the specific content. These distinctions are the submodalities and it is the configuration of these, suggests Bandler, that determines the next element in a sequence or strategy.

To illustrate this, take two different memories, one pleasant and one unpleasant, and picture each in your mind again. Notice how each makes you feel. If the experiences you have chosen are good examples, you should find that the first is followed fairly quickly by a positive kinaesthetic (feeling) and a negative kinaesthetic follows the second. Now, if you compare the submodality configurations of the two initial images, you will find that they are quite different. Use the following list of visual submodality distinctions to help you. This is not intended to be an exhaustive list but does cover the most common visual submodality distinctions. Keep in mind that submodalities are about **how** we represent our experience and not **what** that experience is.

- Brightness
- Contrast
- Colour - black and white
- Distance
- Location
- Associated - disassociated
- Movement
- Depth

On the whole, we do not tend to reflect very much on how we represent the world because most of the time we are just getting on and doing it. For this reason, people sometimes have a little difficulty when they are first asked to do these types of exercises. Take your time over the above exercise; it is well worth the effort. After you first recall the experience, spend a while allowing the image to stabilise in your mind before you start identifying the distinctions. Learning to do this is itself a skill that improves with practice.

Although submodality configurations for particular types of experience are unique to each individual there are certain configurations that tend to be universal. One example of this is in the case of traumatic memories. We shall have more to say about managing trauma through counselling in a later chapter but here we shall look more closely at how submodalities operate in trauma.

Immediately after a trauma, a client will often experience flashback memories to the traumatic events. These memories are most usually represented through the visual and kinaesthetic systems. Within the visual representation, typical submodalities are full association, vivid colours, movement and almost panoramic perspective. It really is a reliving, almost as if the client were there again. If we contrast this with a person who has suffered trauma at some time in the past and successfully recovered, we find a far less emotionally impactful memory. Here, clients recall the traumatic events most typically in a dissociated manner. They see themselves in the memory, often far off and quite small. The visual representation is quite dull and feint and often still. It is almost directly the converse of the configuration in the first example and, as a result is far less traumatising on recall. Through time, the mind naturally and quite unconsciously adapts the memory to make it more acceptable. Time is a great healer and this is one of the ways in which that healing takes place. Of course, knowing this, we can help clients to a speedier recovery by teaching them how to systematically change the submodalities of the memory, the first step being to create the dissociation. This in itself is usually enough to lessen the negative feelings.

You can try this for yourself. You may not have any recent traumas in your life but try to think of an embarrassing memory, one that when you recall it now still leaves you feeling uncomfortable. Picture that in your mind's eye and note the submodalities. It is likely that you are associated; this is what maintains the uncomfortable feelings. So, step out of the memory and watch yourself going through those events again, notice how the feelings change.

Submodalities and learning the skills to manage them and bring about useful change is worth spending time on for both for yourself as the counsellor and your clients. Always start with exploration of what is, and remember the attitude of curiosity we discussed in the previous chapter. There is no such thing as a bad or wrong submodality configuration, they all work wonderfully well to bring about the effect they do. What there is are more or less useful configurations, and helping clients learn about these is the starting point in giving them control.

I want to finish this chapter on subjective experience by exploring a model that helps to provide a framework for all that we have discussed so far. This model was developed by John McWhirter some years ago and like a lot of DBM (Developmental Behavioural

Modelling) models it is a tool for making useful distinctions in the process of building our subjective experience; our model of understanding. It is called the IRCO model and it makes four basic distinctions that can be thought of as stages in the process of modelling subjective experience.

Stage one is the **Input** stage. It is the process of sensing the world and we explored this earlier in the chapter. As we identified then, the process of inputting is not exhaustive – indeed we are quite selective in what we chose to attend to in selecting input. And, as we also stated earlier, inputting is not a passive process. We actively select our input.

As we input through our senses we must **Relate** the input to our existing understanding in order to inform ourselves and make sense of the new input. We may search through memories or construct possibilities in order to make sense of the sensory information we are inputting. Relating can be thought of as the stage where we attempt to understand what our senses are telling us on the basis of past experience. Relating is stage two of the model.

As we relate to what is already known, our new understanding becomes information we can act on in the **Compute** stage, stage three in the model. It is at this stage that we make the decisions on how to react to the new information. In the compute stage, we must formulate our behavioural response and this includes the option of no response at all.

Only when we have arrived at a satisfactory behavioural response can we act and it is action or behavioural response that becomes the **Output** of this process. Output is the final stage of the model and it may be in the form of a specific behavioural response as in some action in the world or it may be a more subjective behavioural response as in making changes to our existing model of understanding.

The final model then looks something like this:

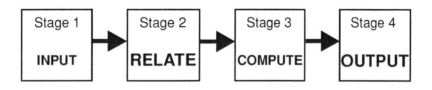

Figure 5

For simplicity's sake, it is represented in a linear manner but it can easily be seen that new output helps determine the future input giving the model a more circular or recursive feel.

The following examples should help your understanding of the IRCO model and in particular its usefulness as a counselling aid.

A client is attending a business meeting with a potential customer. Some of his company's competitors are also in attendance. He believes that the competitors have a better product than the company he works for and this leads to him feeling defensive.

He hears one of his business competitors talking about their product. The competitor looks confident and assured. All of this is available as **input**. Our client focuses on the confidence of the speaker and those aspects of what is being said that confirm his belief that the competitor's product is better. It is this belief, part of his current model of the world that he is using to **relate** the new input to. This serves to reinforce his belief so that when it comes to his turn to speak, he **computes** a defensive **output** where little is revealed about his company's product. As a result of this, his company fails to secure a contract with the customer.

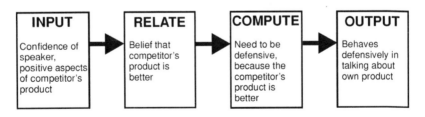

Figure 6

By breaking it down in this way, we can begin to explore where changes might take place; changes that might allow the client to **output** a different response at some point in the future.

Because the client's current understanding at the **relate** stage was influencing the **input** in a less than useful way, changing the current model by widening the criteria the client was judging the products on proved on this occasion to be enough to bring about a desired change. Rather than just concentrating on the positive aspects of the competitor's product, the client was encouraged to widen the scope of his attention to include the negative aspects of the competitor's product and the more positive aspects of his company's product. Now when the client re-lived the experience of the meeting, the competitor's sales pitch was seen in a wider perspective and produced a less defensive response in himself.

In the second example a client came to counselling as the result of relationship difficulties with her long-term partner, which was affecting her work performance. She described her partner as being hypercritical and felt that over the years this had eroded her self-confidence. When exploring a typical interaction, we discovered the following pattern. The client focused almost exclusively on specific, critical comments her partner made about her appearance. This was her **input** from the interaction. She **related** this to her own sense of self, her own self-image that she described as 'drab' and 'dowdy' looking. She **computed** that her husband's criticism was accurate (i.e. it matched her own understanding) and as a consequence and quite unconsciously, the submodalities of her self-image became slightly more drab and dim (her **output**).

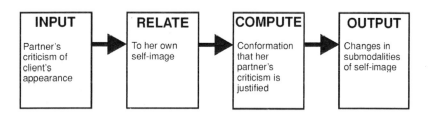

Figure 7

An important aspect of this example is that it shows that output doesn't necessarily have to manifest itself as an overt, recognisable behavioural response. Neither does it have to be within conscious control of awareness. It is an output of the process and not of the person.

This client was eventually helped in a number of ways but the initial focus was on widening the scope of her attention at the input stage so that her partner's negative comments could be balanced with more his more positive comments. Later, she was helped to develop a more positive self-image by changing the submodalities of her internal representation so that she related negative comments to a more positive internal representation of her self.

A client's problems can occur at any of the four stages and indeed often at more than one. Using the IRCO model, we can more precisely and specifically pinpoint the client's problem. Is it a problem with input, is the client simply not attending to the most useful things? Or, maybe it's a problem at the relate stage – the client is not making the right kind of sense of the information she is receiving. She is misrelating it and therefore misunderstanding it. Then again, it could be a problem with her computing – she has the right understanding of the situation but draws the wrong conclusions. And, finally she could be accurately processing the first three stages but failing to make the appropriate output, not acting on her understanding.

Use the IRCO model to help organise your and your clients' understanding of where specifically the problems lie. You will find that the more you use the model in this way, the more you will come to understand its usefulness. Like many of the models used in systemic counselling, on first sight it seems relatively straightforward. However, as you become more skilled in its use, you will develop a greater understanding of the subtle complexities of human understanding. More importantly, you will be less likely to fall foul of a problem many counsellors and clients experience, attempting to make changes at an inappropriate stage of the process. Models like the IRCO model improve your precision as a counsellor.

In this chapter, you have been introduced to some of the theories and models that underpin a constructivist approach to counselling. With this understanding, you will be better able to apply the skills and methodologies covered in the remaining chapters.

4

Developing Sensory Acuity

When Bandler and Grinder embarked on their project of modelling effective therapies in the early 1970s, they discovered certain skills shared by those they modelled. One of these skills that seemed particularly well developed in their subjects was the ability to notice minor and seemingly unimportant details in their clients' behaviour. By developing their senses and their willingness to attend fully to their clients, they made available to themselves a range of information, allowing them to build a more complete picture of their clients' situations. This skill is known as sensory acuity and, like any skill, it can be developed and improved.

Sherlock Holmes was a great fictional master of sensory acuity. He would often confound poor Dr Watson with his observations of minute detail. But, what is less well known is that Holmes was based on a real person, a Doctor from Edinburgh who had amazingly well developed powers of observation. As counsellors, we need to develop the acuity of Holmes, the ability to notice the smallest of detail because, like the detective, a counsellor's job is to build up a picture, and understanding of what is happening – and that requires attention and patience.

John McWhirter tells the story of a client, a young lad from Glasgow who had a remarkably highly developed visual acuity. One of the consequences of this was that he could often tell what colour a person was thinking of simply through observation. It became something of a party trick and his success was much higher than chance would provide. Apparently this young lad came from a very violent background; he had a father who would often beat him and other members of the family for no apparent reason. As a result, the lad became very attentive to the slightest sign that trouble was imminent so that he could escape before it began. His heightened visual acuity was developed out of the fear and the need to survive.

As this story illustrates, the senses are highly sensitive and the level of detail that can be attended to and noticed is often quite surprising. It is often thought that certain people have a sixth sense or even extra-sensory perception because of their uncanny ability to arrive at an understanding of a situation on the basis of what appears to the rest of us to be little or no information. Often these people are themselves unaware of what they are basing their conclusions on but if time is taken to explore the situation with them it is usually discovered that they have noticed things through the usual five senses that have passed others by. It has been shown that many spiritualists, mediums and fortune-tellers base their abilities on heightened sensory acuity although it must be added that they are often unaware of this themselves and genuinely believe they have some 'special' skill.

This ability, often referred to as 'intuition', is culturally and historically considered to be more highly developed in women but it is now clear that men are just as capable of developing heightened sensory acuity.

The reason that sensory acuity is so important in counselling is that it optimises the amount of information available to us as counsellors. Remember we are building a model of understanding of our client and our client's circumstances. We start with a blank slate and our understanding is built upon both what the client tells us and our own observations as we listen to the story. At the beginning, we have no way of knowing what will or won't be relevant, so every little piece of information is potentially important. As we begin to build our understanding, then the pieces start to fit together to give a more complete picture. Sometimes pieces don't fit together and that is an indication that some pieces may be missing – that we need more information.

Training our senses to attend more fully allows for an increase in available information therefore improving the chances that we will arrive at a more complete and useful understanding of our client. In this chapter, we shall explore some ways in which you can develop improved sensory acuity.

When training people in counselling, we often find that novice counsellors spend too much time wrapped up in their own thoughts, theories and speculations and not enough time attending to the client before them. They end up addressing the issues that arise from their own 'fantasies' about the client and not the actual issues that the client is presenting with. This often includes various forms of diagnostic labelling and the imposition of less than useful and inaccurate models of understanding.

The starting point in developing improved sensory acuity is simply recognising and appreciating its importance. Instead of jumping to premature conclusions, counselling students are encouraged to remain open-minded and fully attentive to the clients before them. This shifting of attention from more internal to more external takes time to fully develop but the more its importance is appreciated, the more likely it is that this shift will be made. Attending more fully to the client is the behavioural manifestation of the attitude of curiosity and wonder we discussed in chapter two.

The following exercises are primarily aimed at developing visual and auditory acuity as these are generally considered to be the most useful in the counselling situation. The kinaesthetic sense is also worth developing but for various reasons touch plays a minimal role in counselling. Smell and taste, the two more primitive senses are less important in counselling although people such as wine tasters obviously have these senses developed to a high level of acuity.

Before we begin some exercises in helping you develop your sensory acuity, I want to introduce the concept of calibration which is one very useful way in which we can put our newly developed and heightened skills of sensory acuity to work.

Because mind and body are different aspects of the same whole – at least this is what we are going to assume – then it stands to reason that whatever is going on internally, within our minds, will manifest itself behaviourally through our body. This isn't really too contentious. For example, we are all capable of telling if someone is happy or sad through the way in which they behave. The external body signals for all emotions, especially when they are extreme, are obvious to us all. We can take this further and assume that for every internal mental state or process there will be a corresponding external manifestation. We might not know what this is, it may be subtle or unique to a particular individual, but it will be there.

Often we hear of couples that have been together for many years developing the ability to know exactly what is going on for their partners, as if they can read their minds. Of course this is simply the result of years of familiarity – they learn, often unconsciously, to read their partners' non-verbal signs.

Sometimes we can assume that certain external manifestations of internal processes are pretty much universal. An example of this would be smiling, which normally manifests when a person is happy. Books have been written on the subject of non-verbal behaviour and its meaning and attempts have been made to arrive at more complex and subtle universal rules of non-verbal behaviour and what it represents. However, I want to warn against relying on universal rules because they are often wrong or misleading and certainly they do not respect the individuality of the client. What we must do instead is learn to read the individual and we must start out afresh with this each and every time we begin working with a new client. To do this we must learn to calibrate.

Calibration is the process of setting or establishing a measurement. If we were creating a ruler or tape measure for example, we would need to mark off the measurements by comparing with something that is already known to have those measurements. Only then could we depend on its reliability as a measure. Likewise, if we wish to learn what specific non-verbal behaviour means in terms of internal processing, we need to take measurements or snapshots that can be verified as meaning something specific. We calibrate to a particular set of non-verbal behaviours. For example, we might have a client who sometimes fidgets with his hands in a particular way. We may notice through time that this often occurs when he is talking about something he finds frightening or scary. In other words we calibrate the behaviour to the internal state of fear.

Now, imagine how useful this might be. Using the above example, imagine that we now began to discuss our client's work situation. For many reasons, he might have convinced himself that everything at work is fine but, as counsellor, we notice that each time the office manager is mentioned, the client fidgets in the way we have calibrated as meaning he is experiencing fear or anxiety. What we now know is that there is something about the client's relationship with his manager that makes him nervous, even though he may not be consciously aware of this himself. It provides us with possibilities and options for further exploration.

Unfortunately, there are very few sensory acuity exercises that can be performed alone although some suggestions for practice are included at the end of this chapter. For most of these exercises, you will need to find a partner, friend or colleague to help you. It doesn't matter if they have no interest in counselling, most people find these exercises quite intriguing and a lot of fun. Interestingly, you will almost certainly find a marked improvement in your acuity after just one run through of each of the exercises. They set the mind up to want to notice more and that can only be good.

Think of these exercises as fundamental mind training, rather like a sportsman might work on general fitness in the gym. They are not in and of themselves anything much to do with counselling but they do provide very good training in attending.

This first few exercises are often referred to as 'the mind reading exercises' as it superficially looks as if you are attempting to read someone's mind. Indeed the structure of this is not so very different from the techniques employed by performing mind readers. First you need to find a friend or colleague to do the exercises with you. Then you need to allocate roles. One person will be the subject and the other the practitioner. You should change roles after each round because it's useful to experience these exercises as both the subject and the practitioner. Just follow the instructions below.

Exercise 1

1. The subject identifies two people – one liked, the other disliked. The subject doesn't have to tell the practitioner who these people are.

2. The subject spends a few moments thinking about each of these people in turn. The subject should picture each of them in their mind's eye. When you are the subject, make it clear which person you are thinking of. The practitioner simply observes the subject as they are thinking about each of the people. There should be no discussion during this. What you are doing as practitioner is calibrating to how the subject looks while thinking about each of the people they have chosen

3. The practitioner now asks the subject a series of questions. These questions should be of a type that requires the answer to be either of the two people. So for example, as practitioner, you might ask: 'Which of the two have you known longer?'

   The subject should answer by thinking again of the person who is the answer to the question. The subject should give NO verbal answer.

4. On the basis of observation, the practitioner should try to work out which of the two people the subject is thinking of. The practitioner should state his or her guess and the subject should inform them if they are correct.

5. Repeat with other, similar questions at least half a dozen times each. If you find that you are having no more than 50% success in guessing (equal to chance), then have the subject intensify the representations they have of the two people or chose two people that evoke stronger emotions. If you find you are guessing too easily, then reverse this. Have the subject chose less evocative people.

6. If you find it too easy, set yourself more of a challenge. Aim for some success but also some challenge. Getting some wrong means you will focus even more the next time. Guessing it wrong aids the learning process.

Below are some suggested questions you could ask. Try to create your own to supplement these.

- Which of the two have you know longer?
- Which of the two did you see more recently?
- Which of the two is the older?
- Which of the two lives closer to you?
- Which of the two has the longer hair?
- Which of the two is the taller?
- Which of the two is the heavier?

Now, it's a good idea to compare notes. What sort of things were you observing? Was there one 'tell tale' sign or, was it more the overall look of them that gave the game away? List the types of observations you were making and try to be as literally descriptive as possible. It is useful practice to get into the habit of suspending judgement on what you observe. The more interpretation you read into your observations, the more close minded you become so avoid overly abstract language in your descriptions. One man's smile is another man's grimace. I have listed below some of the things you may have observed. Compare this with your own list:

- muscle tension around
    - the eyes
    - the mouth and lips
    - the neck and shoulders
    - the hands
- skin colouring
- pupil dilation
- eye size (more strictly speaking, how open or closed the eyelids are)
- skin gloss or moisture
- pore size
- breathing rate and depth
- heart rate
- overall posture of head, shoulders and body as a whole
- movements or fidgets of the hands, feet or whole body
- facial ticks or twitches.

You will probably have realised that some of these responses take longer than others to change. For some, the subject would need to think about the people chosen for several minutes for the changes to become noticeable

The next exercise follows the same format but this time the calibration uses the auditory sense.

Exercise 2

1. The subject identifies two different people – one liked, the other disliked. The subject doesn't have to tell the practitioner who these people are.

2. The subject spends a few moments thinking about each of these people in turn. The subject should picture each of them in their mind's eye. When you are the subject, make it clear which person you are thinking of. This time, instead of observing the subject, the practitioner should sit facing away from the subject and listen as the subject counts from one to ten. The subject should count from one to ten whilst thinking about each of the people. So as subject, you will count from one to ten twice – the first time while thinking about the person liked, the second time while thinking about the person disliked. As practitioner, you are calibrating the sound of the subject's voice.

3. Again, the practitioner asks a series of questions that presuppose the answer to be one of the two people. As the subject thinks of the person who is the answer, the subject counts from one to ten again. On the basis of what is heard the practitioner guesses the answers and, as in exercise 1, the subject lets the practitioner know if he or she is correct in the guess or not. *At NO point should the practitioner be able to visibly observe the subject.*

When you have both had a turn at playing the role of subject again, compare notes. Some people find this exercise easier than the previous one, others harder. Much depends on personal preferences.

Compare your list to the one below – it should be similar:

- volume
- tone
- pitch
- timbre
- cadence
- attack/delay
- breathiness
- reverberation
- variability of any of the above.

A similar exercise can be carried out utilising the kinaesthetic sense or sense of touch and although as has already been said, this sense plays a minimal role in counselling it is nevertheless an interesting exercise to experience. When we conduct this exercise in training, people are often quite surprised at just how much information the sense of touch can gather.

Exercise 3

1. The subject identifies two different people – one liked, the other disliked. The subject doesn't have to tell the practitioner who these people are.

2. The subject spends a few moments thinking about each of these people in turn. The subject should picture each of them in their mind's eye. When you are the subject, make it clear which person you are thinking of. This time the practitioner and subject sit back to back whilst holding hands. The practitioner will be calibrating on the basis of the contact between the hands only.

3. Again, the practitioner asks a series of questions that presuppose the answer to be one of the two people. On the basis of what is felt through the hand, the practitioner guesses the answers and as in exercise 1, the subject lets the practitioner know if he or she is

correct in their guess or not. *At NO point should the practitioner be able to visibly observe the subject.*

Again, once you have both experienced both positions, compare notes. Most people find the sense of touch a little trickier than the previous two but there are a small number of people who actually find it easier. Most people are surprised at just how much information there is available through the sense of touch. I have listed below some of the distinctions you may have made. Compare this with your own list:

- temperature
- texture
- movement
- moisture/dryness
- pulse.

This next exercise helps to integrate all three senses into a more meaningful experience. As practitioner you will have the opportunity to calibrate to the 'whole' person as they relate a story to you. Obviously this is much closer to the kind of situation encountered during counselling than the previous exercises.

Exercise 4

1. The subject tells two stories whilst the practitioner observes and listens. Both stories should be about something the subject may have experienced in his or her life. The difference between them will be that the first will be a wholly truthful account of a real life experience whilst the second will be completely fictitious. This is where we get to find out how good a liar you are. Keep the stories relatively short – that way it is easier to ensure that each is a complete truth or complete fiction. As the practitioner, calibrate to what you observe and hear. Obviously, you know which story is truth and which is fiction so look beyond this and notice how the subject looks and sounds different during the telling of each story.

2. Now the subject tells a third story which can either be a completely true account or completely fictitious. The practitioner should not know ahead of time which it is to be. On the basis of what is observed and heard, the practitioner guesses whether he thinks the third story is a truth or a fiction. Clearly the subject needs to put a little thought into the story as a completely absurd story such as alien abduction would be a complete give away.

3. Repeat this a few times until you are able to make clear and conscious distinctions between how the subject looks and sounds when telling a truth or fiction.

Developing sensory acuity and learning to usefully calibrate requires practice and it is suggested that you make a conscious effort over the next few weeks to set aside a little time each day to attend to these skills. Pick situations when you are not required to interact and discover what you can begin to notice once you start to attend more fully; maybe when in a meeting listening to others or on a train or bus journey. Watching people talk and interact on TV can often be a good source of experience for this kind of practice but take care to choose real and not acted interactions; some actors just aren't very good and you'll not learn so much by using them as examples.

One suggestion is to concentrate on a different sense each day, maybe confining this to the main three senses of sight, sound and touch. However, there's no reason not to include taste and smell – after all, when was the last time you really paid close attention to the subtleties of flavour and smell.

In the next and subsequent chapters, we'll begin to build on these skills as we develop a more attentive way of interacting required when counselling.

5

Developing Rapport

The importance of the counsellor-client relationship is something all approaches to counselling share. Indeed for some – most notably the psychodynamic school – the counsellor-client relationship and how the client learns to manage that relationship is the singularly most important aspect. In systemic counselling, the relationship, or more usefully the relating, between counsellor and client is considered to be a means to an end. It is not so much the quality of the relating, rather what can be brought about as a result of that relating.

We refer to the quality of relating as rapport and in this chapter we shall explore how useful rapport can be established with clients. We shall explore the more traditional method of behavioural matching before introducing more recent developments including the use of subjective personal space.

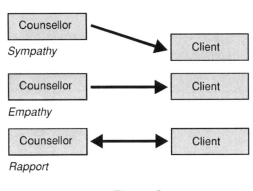

Figure 8

Rapport has much in common with the notion of empathy and to a lesser extent sympathy, but unlike empathy and sympathy, which are both concerned with how the counsellor relates to the client, rapport is concerned with the totality of the relationship or how each relates to the other.

When understanding a relationship in terms of rapport, we have to consider both sides and not just one.

Rapport is a measure of the functioning of the whole system, both counsellor and client, and it is not an absolute value but rather a continuum. At the bottom end is a situation between two or more people where there is zero rapport. At the top end there is such a level of rapport that the people involved are almost indistinguishable. This is because at one level of description rapport can be measured by the degree of sameness between two or more people; sameness of dress, of language of behaviour and mannerisms, of beliefs and values and sense of personal identity; the greater the sameness the greater the level of rapport. A couple who have been together for many years will likely have much in common and therefore share a high level of rapport. It would seem that humans, being social creatures have a great propensity for creating sameness and therefore rapport. We only have to look at the ever-changing world of fashion to see this in action. We see and desire sameness by copying fashion and trends set by others. At the time we feel a sense of rapport with others who are similarly attired although often, when we reflect on previous fashions, there is almost a sense of embarrassment as we ask ourselves: 'Did we really wear that?'

When we first meet new people, we know little or nothing about them. There is little known sameness and it may be that they are very different. As we get to know them there is the possibility that we will establish sameness and if we do then rapport starts to build. We might find that we are of similar age, have similar tastes in music, share similar philosophical and political beliefs and so on. If we don't, then rapport will remain low and we will likely go our own ways.

As rapport builds, a very important aspect of this phenomenon becomes apparent – that there is an increase in mutual influence. The higher the level of rapport between two or more people, the higher the level of mutual influence. From our point of view as counsellors, influence (and our ability to influence) is clearly important therefore gaining rapport must be recognised as a major priority in counselling.

In the 1960s, researchers in the US became interested in the courtship behaviours of unattached young people. Amongst the various pieces of research was one fascinating study that looked at behaviour in singles bars. What was discovered was that there were certain 'tell tale' signs that could be used to predict the likelihood of two people getting together and leaving the bar together; the greater the degree of sameness in overt behaviours and mannerisms, the greater the likelihood of a successful meeting. The researchers noted such things as overall body posture, pace of movement and frequency of sips of drinks. The latter was particularly noticeable. If one of the two people took a sip then the second would often also take a sip until the sipping became virtually simultaneous. Their drinking became matched. We can think of this as being a measure of a high level of behavioural rapport. Of course, at this stage, the couple have probably still to find out how much they have in common in terms of beliefs, values and so on, but this behavioural matching, taking place as it does at an unconscious level, indicates the beginnings of a high rapport relationship. From these foundations, the couple can begin to influence one another and through time increase the sameness.

Bandler and Grinder noticed something very similar taking place between some of the therapists they studied and those therapists' clients. High levels of rapport allowed the therapists to usefully influence their clients; it established a trust that enabled the real business of therapy and change to take place. When they modelled this phenomenon in more detail they found a high level of unconscious behavioural matching. They posed the question 'If rapport is expressed by high levels of matching, can this be reversed; can we achieve high levels of rapport *through* behavioural matching?' After experimenting further, they discovered that to some extent this was possible – rapport could be established through behavioural matching. They had found a short cut to achieving rapport and one that would be very useful to therapists and counsellors. Rapport building is now a standard part of the syllabus for NLP practitioner training.

The following exercises are aimed at providing you with practice in developing behavioural rapport. First though, a few words of warning. Like any unconscious skill, when we make it explicit by bringing it under conscious scrutiny, there is a tendency for it to become ungainly and awkward. For a while, we become a little deskilled. Ask any golfer working on his swing. Behavioural matching is a naturally occurring behavioural skill we all have to a greater or lesser extent. These exercises are aimed at improving that skill although at first they may seem to do quite the reverse as you make yourself more consciously aware of your normally unconscious behaviours.

The first few exercises focus on the non-verbal aspect of our communication. For all of these exercises, you ideally need to work with a friend or colleague. If for some reason you can't, then try practicing them whilst in normal everyday communication with colleagues at work or friends you socialise with. They needn't be overtly involved.

Exercise 1 – Matching and mismatching

1. Whilst in conversation with a friend or colleague notice their overall body posture.

2. Spend a few minutes matching your posture to theirs and notice how this feels.

3. Now spend a few minutes deliberately mismatching their posture. Take a completely opposite posture. So for example, if their posture is stooped and closed, adopt and upright and more open posture. Notice how this feels. Also notice any impact this has on the quality of the relating and the conversation.

4. Finally go back to matching once more in order that you can continue the conversation more comfortably.

Follow this sequence for each of the following areas ensuring that you pay attention to the impact each has on the quality of relating.

- hand gestures and other movements
- breathing rate and depth

- voice volume, tempo and tone
- sentence length
- general pace and tempo of all of the above combined.

Rather like the sensory acuity exercises from the previous chapter, spending just a little time making yourself more aware of behavioural matching in this way will have a noticeable impact how you then continue to make use of matching at a more unconscious level. The next exercise develops this theme further.

Exercise 2 – Matching and leading

1. Repeat the first part of exercise 1. Whilst in conversation, begin by noticing and then matching the overall body posture of a friend or colleague.

2. Now make slight changes and note your partner's response. If the change is not too dramatic, as in the case of exercise 1, you should find that your partner follows the change. If they don't, then go back to matching for a longer period before making the change.

3. Repeat this with the same categories as used in exercise 1.

This is the process of matching and leading and it is the basis of the ability to influence whilst in rapport. If the counsellor leads whilst in rapport, the client will tend to follow that lead in order to maintain rapport. This is a largely unconscious process and it is highly unlikely that the subject will ever be consciously aware that they are being influenced in this way.

Mothers have been using the idea of pacing and leading for generations when 'breathing' their babies to sleep. The mother begins by matching her breathing rate to that of the baby's and then after a while slows her breathing and the baby follows.

It is not just with unconscious behaviours that this process works. It is also fundamental to influencing at higher levels of processing, including beliefs and values. When a client presents with certain limiting beliefs about themselves or the world around them, the counsellor might disagree, offering counter examples and generally trying to convince the client otherwise. However, if rapport is low, the client is just as likely to dismiss such counters, often strengthening their original belief in the process. Better is to match the client's belief before leading him or her into a more useful belief. The following short dialogues between counsellor and client illustrate this point.

Example 1 – The counsellor mismatches the client's beliefs about self

Client:	I'm just hopeless. I'll never be a proper wife.
Counsellor:	Of course you will. Listen you've already told me about how much you do around the house and about how you make sure everything is fine for you husband.
Client:	Yes but that's not enough is it. Deep down I know I'm hopeless.
Counsellor:	You're not hopeless. Look at how well you did through college and in your current job.
Client:	Yes, I was okay at those but now, as a wife ... when I compare ... it's just like ... it's useless.

Example 2 – The counsellor first matches the client's limiting belief before leading them to something more useful.

Client:	I'm quite sure that I'll never be as good as him so there's no point in really trying.
Counsellor:	Yup, I guess from all you've said he is very good and you're only just setting out so you're definitely not as good as him.
Client:	Not as good and never will be. I mean, he's brilliant.
Counsellor:	Yes, well, the way you've described him, I'd have to agree you've a long way to go and you'll probably never be as good as him.
Client:	*(nods vigorously in agreement)*
Counsellor:	I wonder – what makes him so good, I mean it's not the sort

	of thing you're born being good at is it?
Client:	Well no, I suppose he's had to work damned hard to become that good.
Counsellor:	And that's something you can certainly match him on. Hard work. You'll probably never be as good as him in many things but at least you can work damned hard.
Client:	Oh sure, I don't mind hard graft. I work hard.
Counsellor:	And like him, if you work hard at it you're bound to improve.
Client:	Put like that I guess I will.
Counsellor:	So, you want to do that then, work at it – I mean, because working hard is really the best way, isn't it.
Client:	It's the only way at the end of the day. Yes, I can work at it.
Counsellor:	And, even though you'll never be as good as him, you will improve won't you – after all, you can't *not* improve if you work hard can you?

In the above dialogues, counsellor one risks much by taking such a mismatching stance. Not only does the mismatch fail to convince the client that her beliefs are inaccurate, it also puts at risk counsellor-client relationship.

Counsellor two also takes a risk in matching a limiting belief. Obviously care must be taken when doing this. The counsellor needs to know the enhancing belief they are leading the client to, otherwise matching with nowhere else to go could simply reinforce the negative beliefs. This would be a demonstration of empathy but not good use of rapport.

A great exponent of this approach and the use of matching and leading is US counsellor and therapist, Frank Farrelly. In his highly unorthodox approach, Frank makes much use of matching and mismatching to deliberately manoeuvre clients to more useful beliefs. His book, *'Provocative Therapy'* is highly recommended.

Gaining rapport through behavioural matching is an effective and proven way to create the kind of rapport that allows the counsellor to influence the client. However, behavioural matching is often considered superficial, in providing a poor level of rapport. Critics argue that, as it is based on the conscious and deliberate manipulation of the relationship, it fails to create a more profound and meaningful client-counsellor relationship – a relationship built through time allowing trust to develop in more naturalistic ways through the consistent, supportive behaviour of the counsellor.

Much depends on the counsellor's understanding of what is required. To the very many practitioners who practice short term, work place counselling it is enough that they can influence their clients and behavioural matching helps achieve this. They do not normally require – even had they the luxury of time – the type of 'deeper' relationship developed through time.

In recent years, DBM has provided a deeper understanding of the process of rapport and from this we are now able to develop methods of achieving rapport that go beyond the sometimes 'mechanical' techniques of behavioural matching. These newer methods also go some way towards answering the critics of behavioural matching. But, before we explore these, it is worth highlighting the fact that behavioural matching as described above still has a very important part to play in work place counselling.

When John McWhirter returned to the drawing board and remodelled rapport using the tools made available through the development of DBM, he uncovered some interesting ideas about the way we organise ourselves subjectively in the various stages of rapport. The starting point for this new understanding is the notion of **personal space**.

If you consider for a moment the actual physical space your body occupies, you will pay much attention to the boundaries, the point at which you meet the world out there. Everything within this boundary is self and all that is beyond is other – or the world. We relate to and experience the two very differently. Compare the two – first attend fully to self and then attend fully to the world beyond. Now, it's not important that you have words for this but it is useful to note for yourself how the two feel different.

Now return your attention to the boundaries and consider for a moment the degree of permanence or rigidity to these boundaries. Just how fixed are they? Your initial answer to such a question will probably be 'Very fixed, I know exactly what is me and what is not me.' Well, ponder a little longer. At what point does the food you eat become you and not the world out there, and the same for the air you breathe.

If you are wearing shoes right now, try the following little exercise. First, move your toes around inside your shoe. Get a real sense of where you end and your shoes begin. I'm sure you'll feel comfortable with the idea that this is your boundary point. Now, keeping your toes still within the shoe move the shoe around on the floor, feeling the floor through your shoes. Do you not now get a sense of your personal boundary being extended to include your shoe? Indeed when you first try on new shoes, how long does it take for them to stop feeling strange – as if they were not a part of you – to feeling more comfortably part of you.

Gregory Bateson uses the example of the blind man and his white stick. For the blind man the white stick is very much an extension of self, which he uses to sense the world. For the blind man the boundary around self would almost certainly include the stick.

Our sense of personal boundaries is not as fixed as we might first think, and beyond this sense of the physical boundaries of self, we have other boundaries, the boundaries of personal space. Reading this now, pause for a moment and consider the personal space around you – the space which you claim for yourself, the space that if it were violated by a stranger would leave you feeling uncomfortable. For most of us growing up in a western culture, this space typically extends for about an arm's length in all directions. In other words, if someone were to come closer than that arm's length, we would feel that our space was being violated. Interestingly, this is not the same for all cultures. In some parts of Africa for example, amongst the male population, this personal space only extends to the front and not to the sides, meaning that relative strangers can sit very closely side by side without feeling any discomfort what so ever.

Interestingly, as with the sense of physical boundaries discussed earlier, these boundaries around our personal space are not fixed. For example, there are times, usually when we are feeling threatened in some way, when our sense of self extends a little – not to include others but rather to keep others at a distance. There are other times when the personal space withdraws out of necessity – consider for example a busy tube train. Then again, if you drive, you will be aware of the extension of self to include the car. The whole car becomes your personal space and you may well be choosy about who you allow to enter that space.

When in the comfort of our own homes, there is less a sense of personal space in that the whole house becomes our personal space although of course it wasn't always so. Remember when you first visited the house before moving in. It takes a little time for the house to feel like home. When we are with family and loved ones, there is less a sense of personal space as we are usually comfortable allowing these people with our space. We are not necessarily aware that this is what we are doing but essentially we extend our personal space to include those we love. And at times of greatest intimacy, our personal space is perfectly in tune with the person we are with – it is the one space.

Our sense of personal space is not fixed – it shifts continuously and largely unconsciously, according to context. But, what if we were to more deliberately manipulate the personal space around us to either include or exclude others? What impact would that have? If we were to subjectively reorganise our sense of the personal space around us so that, instead of it being a boundary between self and other, it included other and placed a new boundary around self-and-other.

This may sound a little odd but there is nothing mystical about this. Remember back to the earlier chapter on sensory acuity – we said that the senses are far more sensitive than we normally appreciate and, as we discovered, they often pick up on information at a more unconscious level. When we organise the personal space around us, however unconsciously we do this, we give off signals to others around. It's a kind of 'keep out' signal subtlety transmitted through our non-verbal behaviour. As a stranger comes nearer to violating our personal space, so these signals intensify until they have a very definite sense of the space we occupy. This personal space is no longer just a subjective experience, it is now something that is communicated and therefore shared by others.

A few years ago, the author was working with a show jumper. This lady had recently acquired a new horse and this horse was considerably larger and more aggressive that her previous mount. On an early ride, the horse had thrown her and she had now become fearful of it. Of course, this had quite a negative impact on their performances together. Through exploration and application of the ideas outlined above, we discovered two things. First, on her previous mount, the client experienced a sense of personal space that extended beyond the horse to include the horse. She-and-horse were one occupying the same sense of personal space. Second, on the new mount, her sense of personal space was very different – now it was only around herself and excluded the horse. Because of this, her attention was very different. Instead of attending to possible threats and dangers beyond self-and-horse, she was now attending to possible threats beyond herself and these threats *included* the horse. Her horse picked up on this and became ever more difficult to handle. Eventually however, she was able to take this new understanding and consciously and deliberately work at reorganising her sense of personal space to include the horse. Her relationship with the horse and their performances together improved dramatically.

So try the following exercise and lets explore the manipulation of personal space. Read through all the instructions first.

Exercise 3 – Personal space

1. Close your eyes and get a sense of the personal space around you. The space that you feel is comfortably yours.
2. Visualise this space in some way – it doesn't have to be a vivid image just a sense of the space, like a bubble around you.
3. Now experiment with shifting this bubble. Imagine that you can slowly extend it outwards, making it bigger, including more of the space around you. If that space includes other people, notice how you feel in relation to them both before and after you include them in your space.

When you feel comfortable with the idea of reorganising your personal space in this way, begin to experiment a little whilst in the company of others. Sensitise yourself to the impact that reorganising your personal space has on others.

An exercise I often have my counselling students do is using their personal space to include and exclude others. I normally split the group into smaller groups of about half a dozen. I then take one person from each group and ask them to leave the room for a few moments. The remaining group members are then asked to hold a discussion on a subject of mutual interest. They are also instructed that the other member would be rejoining them but, before that, they are to reorganise their personal space to include the members already present but exclude the person rejoining. The sixth members are then invited back in. It is quite illuminating to witness their growing discomfort as they are 'excluded' from the groups. If the group members perform as instructed, the sixth members have considerable difficulty joining in the discussion. After a while, the sixth members are once more asked to leave the room but this time they are instructed to 'include' themselves in the group, to go back into the room and subjectively reorganise their personal space to include the others. This time their attempts at becoming involved in the discussion are much more successful.

The more you practice, the more you will be able to move comfortably in and out of rapport with people whenever you chose because, once you include a person within your space, you have the basis of a good and lasting rapport. Clients will open up more readily as they feel increasingly comfortable with you, trust levels will improve and your ability to influence positive change will also be enhanced. Within the comfort of your personal space, investigation of the client's problem becomes less an interrogation and more an intimate exploration together.

Rapport is essential in the counselling relationship. Without it there can be no trust and without trust there can be no influence. Developing good quality rapport provides an environment in which you can safely explore with your client. In the next chapter, we shall introduce some of the language and questioning tools necessary for effective exploration.

6

Questioning and Information Gathering

'The problem is, I don't really trust the people I work with. Well, some of them, I suppose – but it's not like where I used to work. Everyone got on really well there. You could just say how you felt and no one would be hurt or upset but here, here you only have to say one word out of place and someone gets the hump. And I just hate going to work. I watch the clock, waiting for five-thirty to come around and that's just not like me, not like me at all. I used to get up early and always be raring to go as soon as I got in, but now I suppose I just don't care any more. I know I probably sound really ungrateful, moaning all the time like this. It was supposed to be a better job and I'm getting paid more and everything but If I can't get on with the people I work with, then what can I do? And anyway, because of all this, I've started to get panicky feelings. Not like when I was younger, not that bad. I used to get full blown panic attacks and had to have medication for them but this isn't as bad but I'm worried in case it does get that bad again. I couldn't stand it if that happened. That would be terrible.'

The above is an extract from a client session and was given in answer to the counsellor's question:

'So tell me, how can I help?'

Of course, it's not at all uncommon for answers to even the simplest of question to be lengthy. The above answer is quite short compared to very many given in response to similar opening questions. From all of the information presented in the client's opening account, the counsellor must select, must chose how to progress, where to go next, what question to asks and which area to explore first. These are important decisions and can set the tone for all that is to follow.

In this chapter, we shall take a detailed look at questioning and information gathering. We shall examine something of the structure of language and how we use language as a tool to create meaning and understanding, and how understanding this structure allows us to question and explore with great precision, helping clients build their understanding of themselves and their problems and ultimately guide them towards a useful resolution.

In chapter three, we discussed the constructivist approach to understanding and mentioned that language was one of the tools we used to create our 'models' of the world. In this chapter we shall see just how this comes about. But first a few more general comments about the nature of questioning.

Open and closed questioning

There are two main reasons for asking questions. The first is in order to explore; we ask questions that allow clients the opportunity to tell us more and in so doing rethink their circumstances. The second is in order to direct; there are certain questions that direct clients' attention or their thinking in potentially useful ways.

We can organise our questions into two main types, **open** questions and **closed** questions.

- **Open questions** encourage the client to say more, they open further exploration.
- **Closed questions** normally require a simple yes/no answer and as such they tend to close down exploration. Here are some examples of open questions:

- 'Tell me more about what is bothering you?'
- 'Perhaps you could expand on that?'
- 'How is it that you are in this situation now?'
- 'Could you say some more about where you work?'

Note that these questions cannot be responded to with single word answers such as *yes* and *no* but rather require the client to provide a more in-depth answer. This is ideal for exploration in that it encourages clients to think further about their circumstances and because of this the open question has traditionally been seen as the ideal questioning type for counselling.

Here are some examples of closed questions:

- 'Are you feeling any more relaxed now?'
- 'Do you get on well with your boss?'
- 'Are you happy at work?'
- 'Do you think you are in the right job?'

All of these questions can be responded to with a simple yes/no answer and as such they do not encourage further thought on the part of the client. In answering them, the client will typically close down any further thought on the subject so they do not normally aid exploration. Because of this, closed questions have traditionally been discouraged in counselling and, certainly during the early phases of information gathering, they are rarely useful. But, there is a place for closed questions in counselling.

There are times when it is useful for the client to arrive at certain conclusions about themselves and their circumstances and the counsellor can aid this by the use of appropriately timed closed questions. Take the following example. This is taken from the end of the first session of counselling. The client had entered counselling reluctantly despite admitting that he was experiencing considerable difficulties in both his home and working life.

Counsellor: Okay, well, we need to finish shortly so let's just sum up for
                    now. We've started to explore some of these difficulties and

	you've explained to me as best you can something about what has been happening over recent months.
Client:	Yes.
Counsellor:	Well, I think that this has been a useful start to counselling, I certainly think I have a better understanding of your circumstances than I did. How about you? Do you think it's been useful?
Client:	Yes, yes, I do. It's surprised me actually but already I feel better just from having talked it through.
Counsellor:	Okay, well, we can obviously explore further next time. I'm assuming you'll be coming back next week?
Client:	Yes, I think that would be good.
Counsellor:	So, in the meantime, you just need to think about where you want to take this next. Are you happy to do that?
Client:	Yes, thank you. Yes, that will be fine.

Through the use of closed questions, the counsellor leaves the client feeling positive about his experience of counselling and already looking forward to the next session. Here it was useful to have the client arrive at a definite conclusion and stop any further thought or exploration of these specific issues. This is where closed questions can be useful when we want clients to arrive at definite conclusions and we often use them after a period of exploration. This difference is more technically know as the difference between **divergent** and **convergent** processing.

Open questions encourage divergent thinking and closed questions encourage convergent thinking.

It is also useful to note that not all the questions in the above extract are stated in question form, instead they take the structural form of a statement relying on the intonation of the counsellor to use them as a question (in questions the tone of voice is usually raised at the end of the question.) The very first statement the counsellor makes encourages a closed answer from the client even though it is not really a question at all but rather a statement. Using a statement as a question is often a very good way of asking a closed question. When

69

questioned in this way, the client's response is not always verbalised but the observant counsellor will notice a response nevertheless. Here are some examples of closed questions structured as statements.

- 'Well, we've explored this very thoroughly.'
- 'I'm sure you are glad that you've been able to share these concerns with someone.'
- 'These problems can be overcome.'
- 'You're not sure how to begin to solve this.'

As an exercise, take the example client's response from the start of this chapter and think of at least four different **open** questions that you could use to encourage further exploration. Write these down, as we'll be making use of them shortly. When you have written down your four open questions, think of four **closed** questions and write these down. Explain why these particular closed questions might be useful.

Question calibration

Experienced and competent counsellors will often phrase questions in such a way that they are able to help the client explore the central issues of their problems very efficiently. What practice has provided them with is the ability to **calibrate** to the client's responses to questions so that they have a very clear idea of what type of answer they can expect from any given question. In essence we do not ask a question unless we are fairly sure of the type of response. Clearly we will not know specific content but, if we ask a question about a client's work situation, we would not expect an answer about last year's holiday. We will expect and know that the answer should be in some way relevant to the question. If it isn't, then we need to rethink the question because, as counsellors, it is our responsibility to ensure that our questions are interpreted the way they are intended. So, for example the following question ...

- 'So how are things?'

... could result in a wide range of responses. We would have no accurate way of predicting the type of answer although we could be fairly sure that the answer will involve the client's assessment on the state of something. A more specific question might be:

- 'So how are things at work?'

We have narrowed down the scope of the question so that now we can more accurately predict the type of answer.

Knowing what type of answer you are likely to get in response to your questions, including whether the answer is open or closed, is an important skill to develop in counselling.

Take the four open questions you wrote down earlier in this chapter and next to them write down what type of answer you would expect. Think of such things as level of detail, general content, what the answer might be about and so on.

As a further exercise, sit down with a friend or colleague and ask them to tell you something about a hobby or interest they have. Once they have introduced you to the topic step back and think about what you might ask next. Write some questions down and next to them predict what type of answer you are expecting. This is the start of a calibration process. At this stage, it doesn't so much matter whether your questions are useful or not, just that you have a clear idea of what to expect. Now ask each of the questions and check how closely the answers match the answers you expected. If they are very different, think about how you might re-word your question in order to get the type of information you originally intended to get.

Through time, calibration of questioning can become a most useful habit. Your questioning will evolve and become ever more effective, but you need to be honest with yourself and be prepared to change your questioning if you are not getting the response you want or expect.

The fractal language model

I now want to turn to how we use language to create meaning. And, given that the meaning we create is only one of many possible meanings, we can assess the usefulness of any particular understanding. In terms of our role as counsellor, if the meaning the client creates is the very meaning that creates difficulties, then we can, through understanding how the client uses language, help them create a different meaning, a meaning that helps resolve the difficulties. Once more we do this through questioning but now the questions we devise will be based on specific language patterns identified within the client's responses.

The **Fractal Language Model** is a model of language that offers a way of understanding the structure of language in such a way that we can identify specific patterns in the language we use. These are universal patterns that occur in all language use independent of any specific content. The model has been developed over the past fifteen years or more and is based on earlier work by Bandler and Grinder and before them on the work of linguistic researcher Noam Chomsky.

The fractal language model is subdivided into three sections, each concerned with a different aspect of our language use. These are sometimes referred to as the **Universal Modelling Principles**. The three sections are:

1. Detail
2. Scope
3. Connection

Detail

The first set of patterns is concerned with how we select the **details** of our linguistic representations; what we have included and what we have not included, how much of the detail we have included and how accurately we have represented what is included. For example, if I say 'I went on holiday', there is only so much of my actual experience of the holiday represented in that one short statement. Where I went, how long for, what it was like and so on – these are all details that have not been included. Through first identifying where details have not been included, or included only to a small degree or actually misrepresented, we can then begin to formulate questions that help fill in the detail providing to both our clients and ourselves as information gatherers, a fuller and more accurate representation of the client's situation.

Practicing identifying the level of detail represented in a particular piece of language helps sensitise us as counsellors until the process of helping clients flesh out the details becomes almost second nature. Try the following exercise:

Exercise 1

1. Read through the counselling extract from the start of this chapter.

2. Make a note of the following.

    a. Where a specific piece of detail has not been included. For example in the statement 'I was angry.' Nothing is said about what the person was angry about or who they were angry with. These are details that have not been included.

    b. Where a piece of detail has been included but poorly specified. In the same statement 'I am angry.' The nature of the anger and how it was experienced and expressed have not been specified. The danger here, of course, is that on listening to a client express such a statement, we may fall foul of believing that we know what their anger was like, based on our own experience of anger. We might fill in the missing detail on the basis of our own experience of anger and consequently impose our understanding onto the client. This is what we want to avoid through good questioning.

    c. Having identified the missing details or the partially specified

73

details, think about what questions you might ask to fill in and fill out the blanks. Make a list of these questions.

These questions are often referred to as the **specifier questions** and it is specifier questions that constitute the starting point of any information gathering. Until we have flushed out the details, it is not useful to probe any deeper.

The following transcript demonstrates the use of specifier questioning in response to the client's use of *detail* language patterns.

		Detail language pattern
Client:	I've been feeling very low.	Detail missing – *low about what?*
Counsellor:	What have you been feeling low about?	
Client:	Oh you know, life in general.	Detail unspecified – *life in general*
Counsellor:	Okay, what in particular about life?	
Client:	Oh you know, people - they can be really cruel and selfish.	Detail unspecified – *people* Detail unspecified – *cruel* and *selfish how?*
Counsellor:	In what way are they cruel and selfish?	
Client:	Well, they only want to help you if they get something from it. I always help regardless of how it benefits me.	Detail unspecified – *they* Detail unspecified – *help how?* Detail missing – *help with what?* Detail unspecified – *something*

Notice how the client's answers grow longer as more detail is flushed out. There is still a way to go with this example before the counsellor can feel that she has a reasonably specified description of the client's problem, and questioning along similar lines should eventually result in a much richer understanding. Take care however. Questioning in this way, especially when you start to get more detailed answers, can irritate the client. If handled insensitively, you can begin to sound more like an interrogator than a counsellor. Observe the client's total communication for signs of frustration or annoyance and be prepared to temper your questions accordingly. Above all, remember what we discussed in chapter two. Rapport is of ultimate importance and should not be sacrificed to satisfy the need of more detail.

Nominalisation

There are two specific patterns from the **detail** section of the Fractal Language Model that deserve special attention. These patterns explain how it is that we can talk about ideas and concepts that are to do with ongoing processes or behaviours as if they were real and tangible objects. When we use these patterns to help build our understanding, it is as if we are fixing or solidifying some aspects of our experience that would otherwise be transient and nebulous. By fixing them, we give them a more objective existence and because of this they become more manageable. Here is an example of what I mean. In the statement, 'We have a very rocky **relationship**', notice how the **relationship** is being talked about and represented as if it were an object that existed in the world; that it had some kind of tangible existence. It is being spoken of in a similar way that we would speak of a real object. We could easily replace the word relationship with a real object and it would still make meaningful sense for example in the statement 'We have a very rocky **boat**'. Of course, more accurately, a relationship is not a thing at all, it is an ongoing process. It just helps sometimes to talk about it as if it were a thing. It gives it a reality that helps us feel a little more secure.

The language structure I have just described is called a **nominalisation** and it is remarkably common in our everyday language use. It is an example of where our language misrepresents or alters a specific detail of our experience. Mostly this is useful, but sometimes it is less useful. We'll stick with the example of 'relationship'. If we nominalise *the process of relating* into a separate entity *'the relationship'* then we are to some extent, relinquishing some of our control over the process. Although it is 'our relationship', it exists separately from us and therefore takes on a life of its own. This makes it harder to control. It also becomes fixed, and fixed things are harder to change than dynamic processes. This is all very well if the relationship is a good one. In fact this is exactly what we would want. Because it has this kind of static, external existence, it can take care of itself and we don't have to bother ourselves with it. It's there, it's good and it's relatively permanent.

However, when a relationship is not so good, the very sense of permanence and separate existence that was previously useful now becomes problematic; the process needs to change but its solidity and permanence make it hard to change.

Try the following exercise. First, picture in your minds eye a **relationship** that you have. Now, picture in your mind's eye **relating** to that person. Now, compare the two images you had in your mind's eye. In all likelihood the first image was fairly static, possibly even a still image, whereas the second had more movement in it. You were looking at the process of relating.

The second of these representations is in the **denominalised** form and in situations where a client is holding on to a less than useful nominalisation, the first step for us as counsellors is to help them denominalise in order to have a more accurate and useful representation of the nominalised process. We do this referring to the process in its denominalised form so, for example, if a client were to make the statement, 'We have a poor relationship', we might respond with, 'How are you relating poorly?' Notice that in the main, denominalising simply requires adding 'ing' to the end of the original nominalisation. It is, if you prefer, the turning of a noun that was never really a noun in the first place, into a verb. Here are some more examples.

Nominalised	Denominalised
'We have a difficult relationship.'	'How are you relating with difficulty?'
'I have problems with interviews.'	'What problems do you experience when interviewing?
'I have a problem.'	'What are you finding problematic?'
'He doesn't give a care for me.'	'How is he not caring?'

Go back to the opening counselling extract and look for examples of nominalisation. Think about how you might word questions that help denominalise these and write your questions down.

Just as **nominalisation** transforms a process into a thing, so a similar pattern, **lesser nominalisation** takes a behaviour and transforms it into a characteristic. The process is very similar in that a behaviour is a dynamic, ongoing process that becomes fixed as a more solid and persevering quality. For example, suppose I were to describe my friend as 'a lazy person'. What is this quality of 'laziness' that my friend possesses? Is there really something about his 'make-up' or 'personality' that is 'laziness'?

Or, would it be more accurate to think of this label simply as shorthand. That instead there is no quality or attribute as such but rather, *I have attached this construct of laziness to my friend after experiencing him behaving in a lazy way.* I have experienced the behaviours, and judged them to be of a certain kind but somehow, through the use of language, my description of the behaviour has shifted to a description of my friend. There is such a difference between saying, 'You did that lazily', which qualifies a behaviour, and saying, 'You are lazy', which attaches an attribute to the identity of the individual.

Think of some of the qualities you might attribute to yourself, both positive and negative, and then experiment with denominalising them. Rather as you did with nominalisations, check out how denominalising impacts upon your experience of yourself with these qualities.

Again, there is a positive as well as negative impact of lesser nominalisation. If the labels we have picked up throughout our lives, the qualities we ascribe to ourselves, are positive then representing them in the nominalised form, as was the case with standard nominalisations, fixes the quality as a more permanent sense of who we are or our sense of identity. Having a fixed and solid sense of self is important in that it provides us with a foundation on which to learn and develop. Indeed, even a negative sense of self is better than no sense of self, which is one of the reasons criminals and other socially delinquent people often hold on to their criminal identity despite opportunities to change their ways. In counselling and therapy, you will, in all likelihood, come across the 'resistant' client; the client who despite all attempts at help, will not or cannot make the desired changes. Such clients find it extremely unsettling to lose their negative sense of self because of the vacuum this creates. They literally don't know who they are becoming and this can be more than a little frightening.

The following are examples of common lesser nominalisations and questions you might ask to denominalise.

Nominalised (lesser)	Denominalised
'He's just so selfish.'	'What is it that he does so selfishly?'
'I feel I'm really a nasty person.'	'In what ways are you behaving nastily?'
'People are so cruel.'	'What do you see them doing so cruelly?'
'I'm just so dishonest with myself.'	'How is it that you're behaving dishonestly with yourself?

Once more return to the opening extract and identify examples of lesser nominalisation. Formulate a question that helps denominalise this quality.

Note that even though our questions denominalise, their primary aim is still to gather information and help our clients build a richer understanding of their circumstances.

Scope

The second group of language patterns are concerned with the **scope** of our representation. These include such processes as **quantification** and **qualification**. I might talk about the holiday as being 'lots of fun'. I am quantifying by talking about an amount of fun. I might also talk about the holiday as being 'a very relaxing holiday'. Here I am qualifying the holiday as a particular type of holiday; a relaxing one.

Quantification is as it suggests the scoping of experience according to quantities of things. The following are some examples of the process of **quantification**.

- I have *one or two* problems.
- That will take *several* hours.
- We could do with *half a dozen or so* really good ideas.
- I have *hundreds* of real concerns.

In contrast, qualification, another way in which we scope, is concerned with the qualities we place on the details of our experience. Here are some examples of **qualification**.

- That was an *exciting* speech.
- He was a *very dull* colleague.
- That job is *so important*.
- That was a *confusing* experience.

In order to help our clients build a more accurate understanding, it is useful for us to notice when quantification and qualification are being used and check their accuracy. Like all the patterns, these can be double-edged and when not entirely accurate can lead to a severely impoverished understanding. Here's an example. The client in the following extract had just returned from a training course. It was intended to prepare him for promotion but he had returned feeling very negative about the whole experience.

Client: No, it was really a terrible course. The worst I've ever
             attended, a complete waste of time and money.
Counsellor: What, the *whole* course was terrible; you mean so bad that
             you didn't get anything useful from it?
Client: Pretty much, yeah. Well, there were a couple of days when
             we covered some of the new information procedures that
             were quite good. They could have been a lot better but I
             suppose I got something from them.
Counsellor: So even though the course was mostly terrible, you learned
             some useful things.

The counsellor picks up on the qualifier 'terrible' and gently challenges the way the client has scoped his whole experience of the course with this qualifier. The client, perhaps reluctantly, agrees that some things have been learned and therefore breaks down the full scope of the qualifier.

Here are some examples of questions that can be used to explore quantification and qualification.

Quantification statement	Quantification question
I have loads of problems.	Loads? How many is loads?
There are too many with negative attitudes.	So, how many are we actually talking about?
Getting this job done is going to take weeks and weeks.	How many weeks, realistically?

Qualification statement	Qualification question
That was such a terrible interview.	Was all of it terrible or were some bits worse than others?
He always behaves so pathetically.	He's always pathetic?
I hate having to do that. It's always so stressful.	Is everything about it stressful or are some bits better than others?

Again, look through the opening text and identify the use of quantifiers and qualifiers. Note where they are being used in more and less useful ways and design questions that might help challenge the scope of their use and so provide a more accurate understanding.

There are extreme versions of quantification that are sometimes known as **universal** or **limiting quantification**. Universal when the scope is extended too far as in 'they are all useless', and limiting when the scope is not great enough as in 'I just need one lucky break'. Clearly nothing is ever as simple as the use of these patterns might suggest and if we start to apply them in a negative way to our ongoing experience, then we suffer as a result. Consider the following small exchange between a counsellor and his client:

Counsellor: So what seems to be bothering you?
Client: Oh, everything really.
Counsellor: What do you mean by everything?
Client: My whole life seems a mess. None of my family respect me. I have no friends. It all just seems too much.
Counsellor: Hmm ... that doesn't sound too good. It must feel pretty daunting.
Client: Well, yes, of course, but in a way it might not be so bad. If I can just find a new job, I think everything will work out alright.

This is a language of extremes, a kind of black and white thinking that because it simplifies, offers an appeal to clients who may be struggling to make sense of their circumstances. A way round this is to begin to question the extreme scope in order to create a more complex but never the less more useful understanding.

By challenging the extremity of the scope in this way, we can help the client break down the simplified scoping that has led to negative feelings and reactions and pave the way for building more useful, if somewhat more complex scoping of their experience.

Here are some examples of the use of universal and limiting quantifiers and the types of questions that can be used to explore the client's use of these patterns.

Universal Quantifier	Question
It's all just too much.	All of it? Every single bit? Or are some bits easier than others?
Everyone needs to work harder. They're too lazy.	Everyone? There are no exceptions?
These objectives I've been set, they're completely unrealistic.	They are all unrealistic?

Limiting Quantifier	
If they'd just try a bit harder I'm sure we can get there.	So, is that all that's needed?
What I need is a break, and then I think I could really achieve something.	Just that? Or could there be other things that would help?
The trouble with this company is they won't invest. If they would just invest a bit more in training, I'm sure we could overcome these problems.	So, it's juts about investment. With the right training, things could be turned around. Is there anything else needed apart from that?

Connections

A final set of patterns is concerned with how we **connect** our experience in order to create meaning. We make judgements, such as, 'that was a great holiday'. We connect using cause and effect relationships as in, 'because of the holiday, I was able to relax'. We connect meaning to our ongoing experience and we use language to help create this meaning.

At the heart of our understanding are the beliefs that we hold, and these are formed every time we make a judgement. We make judgements about ourselves, others, the state of our world and so on. Quite often the judgements we make and act upon occur so naturally that we are hardly aware that we are making them. Judging is something that humans simply cannot not do. We might say things like, 'He likes me', or 'I'm not sure about that', or 'That seems like it might be difficult.' These are all **judgements**, the first of the connection patterns we shall be looking at. Any linguistic statement that makes some claim about how things are, how thing should be or how things could be will be a judgement.

Reread the opening client extract and make a note of the judgements made by the client. The truth of some may seem self-evident but others may be more questionable. We might ask ourselves how the client came to such conclusions, looking for the evidence or authority on which the judgement is made.

Here are some examples of the types of questions that help explore the evidence a client might use to support their judgements.

Judgement	Question
She doesn't like me.	How do you know she doesn't like you?
It's a difficult place to work.	What do you base that on?
My boss is terribly indecisive.	Can you give some examples? How do you know he is indecisive?
Our customers just don't know what they want?	What makes you say that?

Notice how challenging these questions are. When questioning the evidence that supports client judgments, we need to take great care that we don't imply disbelief. The example questions above are ideal examples given that there are high levels of rapport and that the client is feeling secure in their exploration. In many circumstances, these would need to be qualified or toned down somewhat. But, the overall aim of uncovering supporting evidence should still be our main concern here, especially if we judge that the client's judgement is limiting in some way.

Here we take the same judgements, only this time show a more delicate way to explore for supporting evidence. Notice that in these examples, before challenging the judgment, the counsellor first validates the client's concerns.

Judgement	**Question**
She doesn't like me.	That must be upsetting. What does she do that lets you know she doesn't like you?
It's a difficult place to work.	Has that been your experience, that it's difficult?
My boss is terribly indecisive.	I guess that makes him quite tricky to work with. Indecisive about what sort of things? Perhaps you could give some examples?
Our customers just don't know what they want?	That must be quite frustrating. Is it that they are indecisive or just that they don't communicate their decisions? I guess what I'm trying to get at is how you arrived at that conclusion.

Sometimes, the judgements we act upon are based on nothing more than what someone else has told us; we simply 'buy into' their judgement. More often however, our everyday judgements are based not so much on the judgement of others, but on the basis of our own experience. We experience some evidence that allows us to conclude the particular judgement. If I were to say, 'my client likes me', it will probably be because of something or other the client has done or said, that for me, equates with liking. Maybe he smiled at me, maybe he gave me a gift. These behaviours – behaviours that I can verify through the senses – have a meaning for me that is liking. This pattern is called a **Complex Equivalence**. A complex equivalence is any set of behaviours that for a given individual, equates with a particular meaning. It is the behavioural evidence connected to the meaning. So, in linguistic form, a complex equivalence will often read something like the following:

- 'He's smiling – that means he likes me.'
- 'I'm not doing very well at this, I must be a bit thick.'
- 'I feel nervous – this must be stressful.'

Each of these could be written in shorthand, something like:

Smiling	=	likes
Not doing well	=	thick
Nervous	=	this is stressful

One side of the equation is the evidence, which equates with the judgement or meaning found on the other side. Just as judgements in isolation can be positive or negative, so equivalencies can be positive or negative. They are neither good nor bad in and of themselves, they just are what we do. Sometimes we will equate usefully, at other times less so. Also, the reliability of the evidence we use to support our judgements can be variable; how much evidence we need before feeling comfortable that we have made the right judgement; how well that evidence supports the judgement – all of these will determine how strongly we believe that which we have judged. In the following example the counsellor explores the equivalencies that underpin a judgement the client has made about a work colleague.

Client: The problem is the woman I share an office with. We just don't get on, never have done, never will.
Counsellor: That's a shame, how come?
Client: Oh I don't know – we're just so different, I guess. She's so aloof and cold. Not at all friendly like me.
Counsellor: I see, so what do you mean by aloof? How did you arrive at the conclusion that she was this way?
Client: Well, she never smiles or talks; well, only if I speak first. She hardly ever looks at me and I find that really off considering we work in the same office.
Counsellor: So how long have you worked together:
Client: About four months.
Counsellor: And in all that time, she's never initiated a conversation, never smiled at you.
Client: Not once.
Counsellor: So, do you ever meet outside work, like on work nights out or anything like that?

Client: No, I never go to anything like that. I don't believe in mixing work with pleasure.

Counsellor: Oh, okay. I was just wondering how she might be away from work, with others around.

Client: What, you think it might just be with me she's like that? That she has some kind of problem with me?

Counsellor: I guess anything is possible; we wouldn't want to rule it out.

The client has experienced his work colleague as not smiling, never initiating conversation and never making eye contact. On the basis of this evidence, he has judged her as aloof. Interestingly, once we arrive at a particular conclusion on the basis of our experience, there is then a tendency for us to only notice further evidence that supports this conclusion. This once more helps keep a complex world simple. The client in this example would in all likelihood find it difficult to notice counter example behaviour in his work colleague because this might undermine the judgement he has made. Towards the end of this example, the counsellor sows the seeds for a possible challenge to this rather limiting judgement.

The process of equating is a pragmatic issue and doesn't necessarily represent the truth of the matter. As long as our judgements are more or less accurate, then we can proceed comfortably within the world. When they are less accurate, then maybe we need to review them. Of course they might be less accurate and yet we do not know this. In such circumstances, we shall continue to blunder around getting into all kinds of difficulties. It is worth, therefore, learning something of how we can help clients review their judgements and the equivalencies they use to support them in order to bring about change. To do so, we need to help them to accept that the judgements they arrive at are only some of the many judgements they could have arrived at. Not doing well on a training course could simply be an indication that what they are learning is particularly hard and nothing at all to do with how intelligent they are. Their feeling nervous could mean that what they are doing is important to them, challenging instead of stressful and that the feeling they have is more a feeling of excited anticipation than nervousness. We can help our clients change the meaning of their experience.

Take the list of judgements you identified from the opening client transcript and checking with the original script, identify where evidence is given in support of a judgement; where the whole complex equivalence is offered. Think about how you might explore this equivalence through further exploration. Where there is no evidence given in support of the client's judgements, think about how you my construct a question that would help explore and uncover the equivalence.

If we back up further into the structure of our judgements, we arrive at some point at which we first made a particular type of equivalence. For example, at some stage in our personal histories, we learned that when someone smiles it means that they like us. This learning was through a process of **Inference**, and inference is the third pattern of the connections section. Often we infer things inductively, that is to say, on the basis of repeated and consistent first hand experience, we eventually arrive at the conclusion that one thing means another. Maybe, through the course of our childhood the experience of smiling was often accompanied by other kind gestures, so we came to realise that 'when someone smiles, it means they like you'. This was the original inference on which we established the equivalence.

Other times we infer on the basis of a more deductive style of thinking; working from already established beliefs. An example of this might be something like; 'When I sit exams, I feel nervous, things that make one nervous are stressful, therefore exams mean stress.' Notice how deductive reasoning has been used to build this particular equivalence. It is based on some experience, yes (feeling nervous in exams), but also on another judgement (things that make one nervous are stressful), and the conclusion is deduced on the basis of these two.

When exploring a client's understanding, it can be useful to explore the original inference that led to a particular judgement, especially when the judgement appears to be limiting them in some way. It is however unlikely that clients will present us with their inferences in their account of their problems and limitations. We will only learn more about the underlying structure of their judgements by exploring their origins. Let's continue with the previous example. Remember the counsellor judged a work colleague as aloof on the basis of her not smiling or initiating conversation.

Counsellor: Okay, you say she never smiles or initiates conversation and I'm thinking that could be for many reasons. I wonder, how did you first come to decide that when a person behaves that way they are aloof?

Client: Well wouldn't you think that?

Counsellor: Possibly, yes, but I think it's more useful for us to look at how you decided that.

Client: Well, I think that's how it is. If someone doesn't ever smile at you then they have an attitude problem. They're aloof, yes?

Counsellor: Well, indulge me a little here. I suppose what I think would be interesting, is for you to say a little about how you first came to realise that when a person doesn't smile at you, that means they're aloof?

Client: Oh, well I don't think that's true of everyone who doesn't smile, but you'd expect a person you share an office with to wouldn't you?

Counsellor: And the fact that she doesn't – when did you first equate not smiling with aloof, in this kind of circumstance?

Client: I don't know really. I guess it feels like I've always known it. But when I really think about it, it was an expression my mother used a lot to describe various people she didn't get on with. Maybe I picked it up from her.

Notice how challenging this particular client finds this exploration. It is a struggle to find a reasonable answer to what appears a fairly straightforward question. This is fairly typical because the very nature of inference is such that we rarely question its conclusions. Many of our inferences are historic and deeply-seated structures and recovering information about them can be quite a stretch. However it can be extremely useful, especially if the inference has had a negative influence and in doing so we begin to cast some doubt on the original connection.

At this stage we have three patterns. These three together form the structure of the connected meaning we make of the world.

JUDGEMENT

I

COMPLEX EQUIVALENCE

I

INFERENCE

To see how these three structures link together, we shall look at one further example.

This client was a middle manager of a large food manufacturing company. The company had been experiencing the bite of depression and placing increasing demands on their staff and in particular their managers. The client was considered good at his job and had been in his current position for two years. Within the six months prior to counselling, he had begun to experience many of the symptoms of stress. He was having difficulty sleeping at night, he was snapping at his wife and children, experiencing feelings of inadequacy and generally feeling anxious and unsure. On exploring the issues, it became apparent that despite his immediate manager reporting how pleased he was with our client's performance, our client did not feel he was doing a good job. This **judgement** was expressed often during counselling sessions, and in several different ways:

'I'm just not up to it any more.'

'I don't know why they keep me on in this position.'

'I don't think I can hack it any more.'

When the supporting structure of these beliefs was explored, it was found that he based them on a set of equivalences about what a good manager should be able to do. Such things as:

'A good manager should meet his deadlines.'

'A good manager should have time for his staff.'

'A good manager should be able to manage his time.'

So in effect our client was thinking, 'Because I'm not doing these, I am not a good manager'. When we explored how he had originally inferred these equivalences, we discovered that many had been formed over a period of time during his early days in management. When asked to consider whether these inferences were absolute – in other words, should a manager always be measured on the basis of these specific criteria or, were these criteria appropriate to that particular time, place and set of circumstances – our client began to realise that different sets of criteria were needed for different sets of circumstances. Times had changed and demands on our client's time were now much greater. The question became, 'what makes a good manager in these new circumstances?' The client had been operating from an out of date set of judgements based on inferences from a completely different set of circumstances. This is not at all uncommon, but through understanding the structure of judgement, we can begin to review our understanding and update it to something more useful.

By judging, we bring meaning to our world. We are able to judge how things are and how we need or want things to be. Our judgements allow us to understand how to proceed in the world and how we would like others to proceed in the world. On the basis of how we judge the world to be, we can instruct ourselves and attempt to influence others. We do this through the process of **injunction** – the fourth of the connection patterns. An injunction is like an instruction or an intention to act. Any one judgement can lead to any number of injunctions and through injuncting ourselves and others, we guide our behaviour. Injunctions are the rules we set for how to proceed in the world. For example, if I judge that I am failing in some pursuit, I might, on the basis of that judgement, create an injunction to try harder. Equally I might create an injunction to give up. Much will depend on other judgements that I have arrived at. I might, in judging that I am failing, also judge that I am not good enough, in which case giving up would seem a more likely injunction. But, then again, if I instead judged that it was simply that I wasn't putting enough effort in, then the injunction to try harder would seem the more likely. Injunctions, like all of these patterns, are neither good nor bad, they simply are. Sometimes they will be more useful and at other times less so. The following examples show some typical judgements and the injunctions that might develop from them.

Judgement	Possible Injunctions
I'm not good enough.	I must learn more.
	I will try harder.
	I'm going to give up and try something else.
My boss doesn't respect me	I'll avoid her.
	I'll prove my worth by working harder.
	I'll take her for a drink.
My staff are lazy	They should work harder.
	They should realise how. fortunate they are to have a job.
	I'll sack them all.
I think that meetings are stressful	I'll avoid meetings.
	I'll plan them more thoroughly, especially the things that might go wrong.
	I must stay calm in meetings.

It is important to realise that just as the judgements we arrive at might be inaccurate, so too the injunctions. Just because an injunction is formed on the basis of a judgement it doesn't follow that the injunction is the most appropriate for the judgement. In the following example, a client has presented with classic symptoms of anxiety and stress. The client has become overly concerned with problems at work and has created injunctions for himself and other that are difficult to act on. The injunctions the client has placed on himself are a major contributor to the anxiety he is feeling.

Injunction

Client:	I can't see things getting any better. I'm just not up to it any more.	
Counsellor:	So what is it you feel you should do about that?	
Client:	I'll have to ask for a transfer – that's all there is to it.	*Self injunction*
Counsellor:	Okay, that sounds quite drastic from here. Is it realistic?	
Client:	Well, it would mean a cut in pay and wouldn't look good on my CV but I don't see I have much choice.	
Counsellor:	And, have you already talked to your manager about this?	
Client:	No, but he'll have to agree to it won't he. I mean he shouldn't leave me where I am if I'm making a mess of things.	*Injunction on other*
Counsellor:	Okay then, do you have any other options?	
Client:	None that I can see. I shouldn't have let it get this far; I should have done something much sooner. Now, I'll just have to bite the bullet and take a pay cut.	*Self injunction*
Counsellor:	I'm wondering if your manager will see it quite that way. I'm wondering if maybe he might have some other options for you.	

Note, the counsellor could have explored the underlying structure of this initial judgement by questioning to find the equivalence but instead has chosen to explore the injunctions. One of the beauties of the language model is that it provides many options. In this example, the counsellor can always come back at a later point and explore the structure of the judgement in more depth.

As has already been indicated, injunctions are usually built upon more than one judgement although often one might be considered as the primary judgement. This would be the immediate judgement that leads to the injunction and subsequent action. Clearly other judgements are involved – if not, then any given judgement would always lead to the same injunction and this is not what we find.

It is often worthwhile to backtrack from a given injunction in order to discover what other judgments might be influencing the injunction. This is particularly the case if, despite injuncting, we find that our clients are not getting the results they hoped for in following their own injunctions. In particular it can be useful to explore underlying, secondary and tertiary judgments that are about the kind of person they believe themselves to be. Take the following example.

Here the client is a young admin worker who is experiencing difficulties with her immediate manager. She is required to work very closely in support of her manager and yet she feels that the work she produces is never to her manager's satisfaction. The counsellor identifies a more deep-seated judgment that has impacted upon the client's ability to successfully follow her own injunctions made at a previous counselling session.

Client:	Things are no better really. I tried all the things we talked about last week but nothing made any difference. I can tell she thinks I'm useless by the way she talks to me.
Counsellor:	Has she actually said as much?
Client:	She doesn't need to. I can see she thinks it and I don't really blame her because she's right. I am useless.
Counsellor:	So, despite all your efforts, nothing worked because deep down you believe you are useless.
Client:	Yes, I suppose so. I knew I should never have taken this job.

Take the list of judgements you identified from the opening paragraph of this chapter, the client transcript, and think about what questions you might ask in order to explore the possible injunctions that might stem from these judgements.

As a further exercise, identify any injunctions that are already present in the client language and think about how you might explore these further. Consider how you might explore the implications of the injunctions or what might follow from them.

When acting on injunctions, we do so in the hope that we can bring about some desired change in our world. We are looking for some concrete effect to result from our actions. What is wanted is some kind of change to occur concurrent with our action. **Concurrence** is the fifth pattern from the connections part of the model. Take a fairly trivial example to begin with. The injunction 'Keep off the grass' is made because it is expected that what will happen concurrently with the injunction being acted upon is that the grass will grow. The grass growing is said to be concurrent with the injunction 'Keep off the grass'.

Keep off the grass + the grass will grow

Notice that little is said about any direct causal relationship between the two. Much of the time, we believe that certain things will happen concurrently with our injunctions without ever being greatly aware of the causal relationship between the two. This lack of awareness is quite necessary in order for us to operate efficiently in the world. Imagine how it would be if every time we wanted to bring about some change, we had to think through the causal relationship between the action and the desired outcome. If some one says something that angers you and you decide to have it out with them, you hope for some kind of desired state whereby they might apologise. Much of how you tackle the person in order to bring this about, the injunctions you operate from, will be based on your accumulated experience. You cannot guarantee that your actions will bring this about and you can only be partially aware of how your actions might cause them to apologise. Superstitions are examples of concurrences that have no known causal relationship. Interestingly many of the injunctive habits we develop are little more than superstitions, in the sense that there is no reason on earth why acting on them will bring about the desired state – we just hope in vain that it will.

In order then to explore the implications of particular injunctions, we need to find questions that will identify what the client expects to happen concurrently. This is simply a case of taking the injunction and feeding it back to the client whilst tagging something like 'and what will happen?' onto the end.

Injunction	**Question to explore concurrences**
I really need to get on top things.	Get on top of things and, what will of happen?
They need to be more considerate.	If they are more considerate, what will happen?
We must meet this deadline.	If you do, what will happen?
I'm going to apply for a transfer.	And, if you do, what will happen?

I have already shown that not all injunctions have a direct causal link with the concurrent expectations. Even when they do, we are often not fully aware of the full causal relationship. This is the sixth and final pattern of the connections part of the language model, '**cause and effect**'. A cause and effect pattern is in some ways a more explicitly 'connected' form of a concurrence. When we operate from a specific cause and effect sequence we are more conscious of the direct way in which the injunction (the cause) brings about the concurrence (the effect). It can often be useful to bring about a greater awareness of specifically how a particular injunction will cause a resultant concurrence. Sometimes, in doing this, we come to realise just how weak the connections often are between the injunctions and concurrence. We can then go on to look at what else might be needed in order to bring about the desired effect.

So, having identified what the client expects to occur concurrently with acting on the injunction, we can further explore the connection by asking more specifically how one causes the other. Sometimes this will be transparently obvious and we won't need to question any further, as in the following example.

Client:	Yup, there's nothing else for it – I have to be more punctual.
Counsellor:	And if you are, what will happen?
Client:	Well it's not so much what will happen – it's what will stop happening *(smiles)*.
Counsellor:	Okay, well, I think I know what you're going to say but, what will stop happening?
Client:	My boss will get off my back. Not about everything but at least he won't be able to have a go at me about bad time keeping.

It is rare however for cause and effect relationships to be quite as straightforward as this example and often it is only when we start to question the client's connections, that the weakness of the cause and effect relationship they are acting on is revealed. By exploring this in more depth, we can begin to help the client identify what else might be needed in order to bring about the desired effect. In the following example, the client has arrived at a plan of action to help her deal with the overwhelming amount of information she has to act on each day. Through questioning, the counsellor helps her realise that simply following her plan is not enough that more is required.

Client: I suppose what I should do is set aside some time each day to review what's happened.

Counsellor: And, if you do that, what will happen?

Client: Well, I'll have a better understanding, a better overview. It will help me plan more effectively.

Counsellor: Explain that a little more to me. How, specifically will setting aside some time to review lead to those things happening?

Client: Well, clearly that isn't everything. I mean, it will depend on how well I review, you know. But, if I go about it in an organised fashion, I don't see how it couldn't lead to a better understanding.

Counsellor: Well, it sounds like a good plan but if I can just play devil's advocate for a moment, what if you just get more confused. I'm wondering why spending more time reflecting or review necessarily leads to better understanding.

Client: Well no, when you put it like that it doesn't. Maybe I need to think a little more about how to go about reviewing.

Counsellor: Yes, I think that's a good idea. Because if you don't and you just set aside some time and all that happens is you end up going around in circles like you did before, then I think you'll very quickly get fed up with reviewing.

Client: Yes, you're right. *(long pause)* Any suggestions?

For the final time, read through the opening text and identify any concurrent or cause and effect relationships used by the client.

Consider the strength of the causal connection. Is the cause strong enough alone to bring about the effect or would other causal injunctions need to be identified?

This then is the complete connections model. On the left hand side we have the structure of our judgements and on the right hand side we have the direction these judgements are intended to take us in.

Connections

Judgement X	⟶ And this leads to self/other doing what? X → A	**Injunction A**
↑ How do you know X?		↓ And what will happen if you A?
Complex equivalence X=Y		**Concurrence A + B**
↑ How did you first decide that X = Y?		↓ How specifically does A cause B?
Inference X→Y		**Cause + effect A → B**

Figure 9

By using this model and identifying the patterns within the client's language, you will be able to help them explore a more useful understanding and on the basis of that, more useful ways to proceed in tackling their problems and difficulties.

I want to finish the chapter with a final example that pulls together all the aspects of the connection section of the language model and shows the exploration of the structure of the client's understanding and the establishment of more useful injunctions. As you read through use the connections model to track the counsellor's exploration.

Client:	Well it's all a bit of a mess really. They think they can do pretty much as they please and I'm having quite a job confronting them with it.
Counsellor:	Okay, well, before we get into that tell me more about what it is you think they are doing.
Client:	Well they're taking advantage really. You see, when I started, I was warned that they were a difficult lot to manage so I tried really hard to be relaxed and tolerant, you know, I thought I'd try and win them over. We used to go out for drinks together – that sort of thing. So now, I suppose they don't so much see me as their boss than as their mate and think they can do what they like.
Counsellor:	Okay, how do you know they think that way?
Client:	Well they must do otherwise they wouldn't behave the way they do. They do whatever they like so therefore they must think that it's okay.
Counsellor:	Okay, that seems a reasonable conclusion to make doesn't it?
Client:	Well, obviously it's a bit more complicated than that. There are ringleaders, they think that way. I think a lot of the others don't really think about it at all – they just follow the ringleaders.
Counsellor:	Okay, well, let's come back to what you said at the beginning. You've decided they need confronting.
Client:	Well, yes, that seems the obvious thing to do but I don't much like the idea.
Counsellor:	Okay, let's suppose you do manage to confront them. What do you hope will happen if you do?
Client:	Well, I'm hoping they'll realise what's been happening and buckle down to some serious work for a change.
Counsellor:	Well that makes sense. How exactly will your confronting them bring about this change, this buckling down?
Client:	Well I guess that depends on how it's done. I think what is stopping me is that they'll just become resentful and cause me even more problems.

Counsellor: Yes that could be a danger I can see that. So just confronting them isn't enough. I'm wondering how you might do that without causing resentment?

Client: It's really the ringleaders, just a couple of them, really. I think if they could be brought to heel, the others would follow. If I just had a go at all of them, then I think I would have problems, so maybe I need to focus on the ringleaders.

Counsellor: So if you just confront the ringleaders, you won't get any resentment – is that what you are saying?

Client: Well no, obviously not. Not quite that simple. I think if I did that, then the ringleaders might feel resentful. They might accuse me of victimisation or something.

Counsellor: Well I guess they might. I'm not really sure how things work in your department but if you feel that is a risk that you're not prepared to face and see through, then maybe confrontation isn't the answer.

Client: Well, yes and no – I mean, that's what's stopping me, isn't it. Maybe you're right – maybe I need to have a more informal talk with them, as individuals. Explain my concerns in a friendly kind of way.

Counsellor: And if you do that you think they will stop taking advantage?

Client: Mmmm … I'm not sure. I think the problem is they might not take me seriously if I'm too relaxed about it. What I need is something in between.

Counsellor: That would seem a good idea.

7

Communicational Presuppositions

During the early development of NLP, a collection of interesting and sometimes controversial communicational presuppositions were established. In many ways these presuppositions are the nearest NLP has to an underlying philosophy. They were not original but rather gathered together from various fields of psychology and philosophy including cybernetics, gestalt and constructivism. Over the years, they have been further refined and the ones presented here are based on John McWhirter's version of the NLP presuppositions.

Through modelling expert communicators, the developers of NLP found that many of these presuppositions were held as beliefs by the experts and were clearly manifest in their behaviour irrespective of whether or not they openly claimed to hold these beliefs. They are beliefs that underpin behaviour and are therefore sometimes called 'operational' presuppositions because they influence or operationalise behaviour. Suppose we were to study someone's behaviour – someone recognised as an excellent communicator – and then ask the question, 'what kind of beliefs would a person need to hold in order to communicate so effectively?' We would probably come up with a list very similar to the one presented here. Interestingly, no one has ever tried to demonstrate the truth of these presuppositions, at least not in an absolute sense, the point being it is really of no concern whether they are true or not, what matters is that we behave as if they were.

For each one, I have included a short transcript demonstrating the application of the presuppositions in practice.

1. People operate out of their internal maps and not directly on their sensory experience

This first presupposition is based on a Constructivist viewpoint. That is we each construct an internal map or model of the world based on (but not the same as) the sensory-based experiences we have. Through a process of abstraction, we build meaning from our sensory experience and this meaning then impacts on how we sense the world; how we select what to attend to from the vast amount of data available to us. Humans actively seek out experience on the basis of the beliefs and values they hold – when counselling, it is important to keep this in mind. The client will present you with their 'version' of events and not an objective account of the events themselves.

In Practice
In this example, the client has just received a negative appraisal. Because the appraisal didn't go well, the client became understandably upset. However, by being upset, the client didn't pay full attention to what was said and has been left with an understanding of what is needed that is less than useful.

Counsellor:	So, how did your appraisal go?
Client:	Oh, not very good. I didn't expect it to. I knew he'd be quite critical and he was.
Counsellor:	Oh, so what did he actually say?
Client:	He said he thought I wasn't performing well enough and I have to work harder. I don't know how because I try as hard as I can and put in loads of hours.
Counsellor:	So he actually said you should work harder?
Client:	Well, not exactly, no. I don't think he actually said that but he did say that on current performance, he didn't think I was up to the job.
Counsellor:	But not that you should work harder?
Client:	Well no, but I could tell that's what he meant.
Counsellor:	Okay, but surely he sees how hard you try and how many hours you put in.

101

Client: Well, yes, now that you come to mention it, he did say something about being pleased with my overall effort. I don't suppose I was really paying attention though. It was just too upsetting.

Counsellor: Well, that's understandable. But I am wondering if maybe we need to think a little more about what you really can do to improve your performance.

Client: I don't know. He said something about a training course in the new operating system but I don't know where I'm supposed to find the time for that.

Counsellor: Maybe you need to step back a little and think a bit more objectively about this. If your manager suggested some training, surely he will be prepared to give you the time to complete it.

Client: Well, I suppose so, yes.

2. People make the best choice for themselves at any given moment

Sometimes clients make choices in life that, to a more objective outsider, seem quite hopeless. However, it is important to keep in mind the idea that for them, on the basis of their understanding and experience, the choices they make are the best they can; they are always doing their best to improve their situation. No one knowingly makes a bad choice. The choice they make may seem bad to others around the – to the family, friends and colleagues – but at the time they make that choice, they have no other alternatives. Often others may suggest better alternatives but if the client is unable to act on these, they were never really available as options.

In Practice

The client in this example is undergoing a disciplinary action as a result of losing his temper with his boss. According to the client, this outburst came about as the result of continuous verbal bullying and criticism from his boss. Although he didn't resort to the use of physical violence, he did make several threats.

Client: I hate it that I let myself down like that. People keep asking me why I didn't just ignore him.

Counsellor: So why didn't you?

Client: Well it's not as if I didn't try. But, he'd been going on at me all morning and in the end I just lost my rag.

Counsellor: So you knew you should ignore him, like everyone keeps telling you, but you chose not to?

Client: Well it's not like I really chose not to. I kind of lost control. I'd kept my mouth shut all day but it wasn't just that day, this had been going on for weeks. I just couldn't help it.

Counsellor: Okay the first thing then is that if you really couldn't help it then there really is no point in giving yourself a hard time for not ignoring him. It doesn't matter what everyone else says they weren't there.

Client: Well if only it were that simple but if I had ignored him I wouldn't be in this mess would I. If I'd just kept my trap shut then it would have blown over.

Counsellor: Would it? What would have stopped carrying on just as he had before?

Client: Well nothing I suppose. I just can't help feeling I've let myself down.

Counsellor: You're human. Maybe you should stop being so hard on yourself. The point is, you can't change what has happened. It happened and no amount of wishful thinking is going to make that any different.

Client: I know you're right. I should try and get over it.

Counsellor: Well, there is one thing. You talk as if these were the only two choices available. You either ignore him or you get angry with him. I'm wondering if there might be some other way you can respond. In case this sort of thing ever happens again.

3. The positive self-worth of the client is held constant

Irrespective of the specific behaviours and indeed intentions that the client acts upon, the counsellor maintains a positive view of the client. A distinction is made between self, intention and behaviour. This helps both the client and counsellor explore unwanted or less than useful behaviours more objectively, without the client's sense of self being threatened. The counsellor makes a clear and obvious separation between the client's sense of self and his or her intentions and the way in which he or she behave. Only if the counsellor truly believes there is a difference, will this difference be communicated. This is very closely related to the last presupposition. We have to believe that when clients make choices and act in the world, they are doing so for positive reasons. Even if these reasons are not readily apparent, they will exist if we are prepared to explore in greater depth.

In Practice

This client works for a training agency. She recently attended a meeting with prospective clients where her job was to secure a lucrative training contract. Unfortunately, the prospective clients were not convinced as a result of her presentation that the training agency were capable of providing what they needed and the contract was lost. Since then, her colleagues have blamed the client for this loss.

Client: I made a complete mess of it and the problem is they all think I did it on purpose.

Counsellor: Why would they think that?

Client: Well, they knew I was never really on board with the whole idea. I'd said so often enough.

Counsellor: So, did you do it on purpose?

Client: No, of course not. Well, not like that any way. I mean, I suppose in a funny kind of way I didn't sell the idea as well as I might but that was only because I just don't think we're up to that kind of project right now.

Counsellor: So, you had real and genuine concerns about your ability to provide the service you were supposed to be selling?

Client: Well, yes, I mean, it's not as if I'd not told them. I've been around here a long time and I know what we are capable of. This was beyond us.

Counsellor: So, even though you really did mess up, it was only because you really didn't think you were up to the job. You were really only trying to protect them.

Client: Yes, except they don't see it that way.

Counsellor: Well, we can't help what they think right now but at least we
               both understand that you were acting out of their best
               interests.

4. The explanation or metaphor used to relate facts about a person is not the person

On first meeting a client, the counsellor embarks upon some form of
more or less formal assessment in order to arrive at an understanding.
It is important that this understanding is not confused with how things
actually are for the client. If we become too bonded to our theories or
understanding of the client, we may become closed to contradictory
information, responding to our understanding of the client rather than
the client themselves. It is also important to recognise that clients will
also have their own explanation, which is also not to be confused with
how they actually are. It would be tempting to think that if clients
think something is the case, then it must be so but the clients theories
about their problems and issues are just as likely to be wrong as our
own.

In Practice

The client has been told by a manager that he is 'not creative' enough
to fulfil his current job responsibilities. The client has much respect
for this particular manager and because he values the manager's
views, accepts his views without question. The client now believes
that he is 'uncreative'. This is a theory or understanding he has about
himself.

Counsellor: So, you now believe you are uncreative, is that right?

Client: Well, yes, that's right. I suppose to someone like Tom *(the
               manager)* it's pretty obvious – I just don't know why it's taken
               so long for me to realise.

Counsellor: Okay, so how do you feel as a result of this realisation?

Client: Pretty awful actually. I mean it's made me question what on

	earth I'm doing in this business in the first place.
Counsellor:	And yet you've always been quite successful in the past. You've achieved quite a bit.
Client:	Well, yes, but not without a lot of help from the other guys. I suppose when I think back, it was always them that did the more creative parts. I'm just a slogger.
Counsellor:	Well, sometimes when we learn something new about ourselves, it leads to us re-evaluating the past in light of the new understanding. Sometimes we even remember differently. Are you quite sure that was all you were? I seem to remember you talking before about some really quite creative contributions you made.
Client:	Mmm, I'm not so sure now. It's all a little confusing really. I suppose I did always think that I was being creative but now I'm not so sure. Tom's rarely wrong you know.
Counsellor:	Well, maybe it's just not quite so black and white as you are currently seeing it.

5. Respect all messages from the client

During most of our everyday communication, the component we are most aware of and play most attention to is the linguistic content, the actual words spoken and their meaning. That is not to say however that other communication is not occurring – be it largely outside our awareness. This, often referred to as non-verbal communication, is a powerful and important channel of communication. Studies in the 1960s show that when communicating emotion, as much as 83% of the communication is performed non-verbally. Sometimes there is a contradiction between the verbal and non-verbal communication – this is known as incongruity. It is important to keep in mind that both sides of this incongruity are valid communications that should be respected. It is not that one is right and the other wrong, both need to be respected and responded to. Multi-level attending and communication is a skill that needs much attention and development and, as we saw in earlier sections of this book, these are skills that can be developed.

It is not enough simply to be able to recognise incongruities and certainly confronting clients with their incongruities is both disrespectful of their total communication and damaging to rapport.

In Practice

The following client is a newly promoted manager. He has come to counselling to help with a problem he has recently been experiencing in dealing effectively with certain members of his staff team. In particular he finds some of the more experienced team member difficult to handle and feels that he doesn't have their respect.

Counsellor:	So, this has never been a problem before then?
Client:	No, no, not really. Well, of course I've never been in a position like this before. It's not really a huge problem but I do need to sort it out.
Counsellor:	Well, perhaps you'd like to explain in a little more detail.
Client:	Okay, it's really just about how to handle certain situations. I suppose I just need some coaching really because I've never come across this sort of thing before. There are certain members of the team who have been around for quite a long time and they always seem to know what's what and don't really think they need managing.
Counsellor:	Well do they?
Client:	Not all the time, no, but there are some changes I'm trying to make and they are not too keen.
Counsellor:	They're sabotaging you?
Client:	Oh no, nothing quite as serious as that. It's not all of them either – just one or two.
Counsellor:	Any one in particular?
Client:	Well, I suppose there is one guy. He's worked for the company for twenty odd years. I suppose you could call him the ringleader. He always has an opinion on everything and doesn't seem to respect my position at all.
Counsellor:	I see, and this ringleader, does he intimidate you, make you feel nervous at all? *(The counsellor has noticed the client become quite tense whilst talking about this man.)*

Client: No, it's not that bad. He really doesn't bother me in that way. *(The client clenches his hands together and hunches his shoulders as if guarding against something. His vocal tone has gone up somewhat and there's a tightness to his voice)*

Counsellor: Okay, so he doesn't bother you but you would like some help in learning how best to deal with him.

6. Teach choice – never attempt to take choice away

No matter how negatively our clients or we judge specific behaviours, responses, beliefs or values, we can never be certain that they will not at some point in the future prove useful. We should always attempt to leave clients better off than we found them – at the very least we should leave them no worse. From this it follows that we should never attempt to eradicate behaviours or responses but rather teach or help the client develop alternatives alongside current behaviours. In some forms of traditional psychotherapy, in particular behavioural psychotherapy, new behaviours are often substituted for old. It is our belief that this impoverishes the client.

In Practice

A twenty seven year old project worker came for counselling for help with 'shyness'. He felt unable to react spontaneously in groups of people in case he made a fool of himself and felt that this was getting in the way of him progressing in his current work team.

Client: It's like I always have to analyse everything first. I can't just come out and say the first thing that comes to mind.

Counsellor: Okay, and what is it you don't like about this; about the way you currently are?

Client: Well I must seem really slow to others. I know I'm not but they probably think I need to smarten up my ideas.

Counsellor: So what does it do for you, this analysing? How does it benefit you?

Client: It doesn't do anything for me. I just want to stop doing it and start being more spontaneous.

Counsellor:	What, all the time? In every situation?
Client:	Well yes, people seem to like that in a person. They certainly don't like it if you never say much and just spend all your time thinking about what's been said.
Counsellor:	So, you can't think of any situations where thinking and reflecting on things before speaking might be useful? It's best to be spontaneous in every situation? *(Long pause)* You see you're reflecting now and that's a good thing in this situation because the question was an important one and you wouldn't want to be flippant about something like this would you?
Client:	Well, no, I suppose not. Yes, I guess there are some occasions when it might be good to hold back a bit. But not all the time like I do now.

7. The resources the client needs lie within their personal history

By resources we mean the specific experiences, qualities and behavioural responses the client needs in order to bring about change. Throughout our lives, we experience a vast variety of differing behaviours and it is these we can draw upon in bringing about change. Often the client does not make the connection between past behaviours and the current requirements for a specific problem, it is therefore our duty as agents of change to help the client identify those resources. For example, a client may be experiencing severe anxiety in interview situations but on exploring the client's past, we discover that they have performed very confidently on stage in amateur dramatics. This is an experience that can be used as a resource in helping them overcome interview nerves. Alternatively it may be that even if clients have no specific experiences to draw upon for a particular problem, they can create these through imagination or identification with dramatic roles they have seen on film or TV.

In Practice
This client believed that her indecisiveness in the job situation had cost her promotion and came to counselling to help her become a 'decisive kind of person'.

Counsellor:	So, you actually think you can't make decisions at all?
Client:	Oh I just don't know any more. It seems like that, certainly since the interview. It's like I have to double check everything and even then I much prefer it if the decision is taken out of my hands.
Counsellor:	So this is what, all decisions?
Client:	Well no, not really all. Just the important ones. I worry about them and it all goes around and around in my head in a vicious circle and I can't decide.
Counsellor:	Okay well let me ask you. Is it just at work where you can't make important decisions?
Client:	I'm not sure, how do you mean?
Counsellor:	Well, you mentioned before that your eldest child started school a little while back and I'm wondering how you decided which school to send him to.
Client:	Oh well that's different. I mean I obviously had to decide but that's home that doesn't really count.
Counsellor:	Yes but it was never the less a very important decision.
Client:	Well yes of course.I mean far more important than anything you have to decide about at work. Your son's whole future rests on that decision.
Counsellor:	Well yes it was an important decision.
Client:	So we know then that you do know how to make important decisions. It's just that you haven't been using your decisiveness at work.

8. Meet the client at his or her model of the world

This really stems from the ideas on rapport we discussed in an earlier chapter. To help clients move on and make changes, it is important that we start where they start, with a real appreciation and respect for their current understanding. If we mis-match this, then we will be struggling from the very start, running the risk of polarising the clients and strengthening their current understanding. We might not agree with all they say but we have to accept that this is the starting point before leading them to a more useful understanding.

In Practice

Here the client believes that his new boss no longer wants him. The counsellor begins the session by accepting the client's views on this.

Counsellor:	So, I understand you have a new boss.
Client:	Yes, that's right. He started two weeks ago.
Counsellor:	And your concerns have grown since then.
Client:	Well, yes. I mean, he made it pretty obvious from the start really.
Counsellor:	I'm sorry, he made what obvious?
Client:	Oh, that he didn't think I was right for the team. That he wanted rid of me.
Counsellor:	Oh, I see. Has he told you this then?
Client:	He doesn't need to. It's pretty obvious from the way he's gone about things. He's not asked my opinion on anything. He hardly seems to have any time for me at all.
Counsellor:	That must be upsetting for you.
Client:	Well, you know, I've been there a long time and the old manager, well, he always wanted to hear what I had to say about things.
Counsellor:	So, this new manager, he's different then. He doesn't seem to want you around or value your opinion on things. Where does that leave you?
Client:	I'm not at all sure. I've been looking around, you know. Looking for positions in other departments.
Counsellor:	That's good. At least you're keeping your options open. I wonder, have you spoken to the new boss yet, about this?
Client:	Oh, he just seems far too busy getting to grips with his new job. I thought it best to give him some space.
Counsellor:	Good idea, you wouldn't want to put more pressure on him, I guess he's already under enough. But, I suppose you are going to have to have this out with him sooner or later.
Client:	Yes, I know. But, it isn't just that. I suppose I'm a little scared really.
Counsellor:	Scared?
Client:	Yes, scared. You know, in case he tells me what I don't want

to hear.

Counsellor: Well, there's only one way to know for sure I guess. And, at least you've prepared yourself for the worst. Just think how bad it would have been if you hadn't suspected anything and it just came out of the blue.

9. A person can't not communicate

People communicate at many different levels. There is more to a communication than the meaning of the words spoken. There are the various intonations of voice, gestures, posture and other non-verbal communication. Even when silent, a person is communicating something. The angry child who meets questioning with sulky silence is communicating plenty. When questioned, clients will often take a while to make a verbal response as they search through their experience and reason internally to find an appropriate answer. As they do this, there will be outwards signs of their processing and these, to the attentive observer, are communications. Recall what we discussed in the earlier chapter on sensory acuity. All communications need to be respected as significant.

In Practice
This client has an important decision to make about his future and is struggling to arrive at the best option. Amongst other things he has come to counselling for help with this. In this session, the counsellor puts the options to the client and observes the response. This gives the counsellor clues as to how to proceed.

Counsellor: Okay, so the way I see it you have these two options. You could take the promotion and move away from home. That would be a really good career move and the increase in pay would be a big bonus. Alternatively, you could stay here where you would be close to your family and in particular your fiancé. Your career would suffer but your personal life would be a lot more satisfactory. So, what's it going to be?

Client: (*The client takes a long time in answering and,, whilst waiting,*

> *the counsellor observes a growing agitation. Every now and again the client shifts position, facing one way for a while before turning to face the other. Her hands fidget in her lap in a kind of rhythmic dance turning first one hand palm up and then the other. There is symmetry to her non-verbal behaviour. Finally she answers)* That's just the problem isn't it. I don't know what to do for the best. I just can't decide.

Counsellor: Well, I can see that which ever decision you took as things stand you'd be in two minds about it. I suppose what we need to arrive at, and I really don't know which choice is for the best, is some decision that you can commit yourself to more fully.

Client: Yes, that's what I need.

Counsellor: At the moment, I think both options have equal merit in your opinion. And, both have equal if not the same drawbacks. *(The counsellor is basing his assessment on what he observed earlier. The symmetrical way in which the client responded non-verbally whilst considering the options. He is also attending closely now as he makes this statement for signs of agreement from the client.)*

10. One of the meanings of your communication is the response that you get

Communication involves at least two people. There is a sender and then any number of receivers. What this presupposition highlights is that the responsibility for ensuring the meaning of a communication is the same as the intended meaning is with the sender. For good and effective communication to take place, the meaning of the communication for the receiver should be the same as that which was intended by the sender. All too often we come across the situation where the receiver is blamed for misunderstanding the communication when in fact the sender was not clear in his or her communication.

In Practice

In this example, it is the client herself who takes the blame for misunderstanding the counsellor. The client has come for help after suffering a loss of confidence in her job as manger of a notoriously difficult department. The session opens with the counsellor rather clumsily attempting to sum up the problem, as she currently understands it.

Counsellor: So, you're struggling, the department is not functioning as it should, deadlines are not being met and productivity is low and that's your fault because you're just not up to the job.

Client: Well, when you put it like that then, yes, I guess it must all be my fault. I should never have taken the job in the first place.

Counsellor: Mmm, I think you misunderstood me. I'm not saying that it is your fault – I was simply feeding back to you what I understand you to understand. That is, you think you're not up to the job.

Client: Oh I'm sorry I seem to be doing that a lot lately. Not really listening to what people are saying and getting the wrong end of the stick.

Counsellor: Hey, don't be so hard on yourself. It was my fault – I should have been clearer. Let me see if I can put it another way. At the moment you think that you're not up to the job and that this is the reason that the department is performing so badly.

Client: Yes, yes that's right That is what I think.

11. There are no mistakes in communication, only feedback

This follows on from the previous presupposition and is based on the idea that communication is not a fixed thing of fixed duration but rather an ongoing process. As the sender of a communication, you can never be fully sure that your communication has been understood in the way you intended, but you will receive feedback both verbally and non-verbally that will help you adjust your communication as necessary. That is assuming that you are open to such feedback. It is most useful to take the view that if your communication has not been understood in the way you intended, you have not failed, rather you have feedback that you haven't yet got the desired response. You can now adjust your communication accordingly.

In Practice
This client is recovering from an episode of clinical depression and has recently started back at work in his role as a senior technical advisor. He is questioning whether he should continue with his current responsibilities as he feels it was these, as much as anything, that led to his depression. In this session, the counsellor is trying to communicate that there may have been other factors involved but initially her communication is falling on deaf ears.

Client: It's crazy really, isn't it? I know I have to work but coming back into this when it was this that started it all off in the first place.

Counsellor: I'm not so sure. From all that you've told me, it would seem that there was an awful lot going on in your life that played a part.

Client: *(The client is staring down at the floor and fidgeting in rather an agitated manner. He looks preoccupied.)* I mean, I'm in exactly the same office, with the same people and the same duties. Nothing's changed so what's to say I won't just become depressed again.

Counsellor: I can see how you are really concerned about this. I guess that's normal for anyone in your position. But so much has changed in the rest of your life since then. All sorts of difficult things were going on back then and a lot of these have now been resolved.

Client: *(The client continues to fidget and stare at the floor.)* It wouldn't be so bad if they gave me a different office or something. Somewhere where I wasn't always reminded.

Counsellor: Robert, listen, I need you to do something for me here. Can you please lift your head for a moment and listen very carefully to what I'm going to say. *(The client slowly lifts his head and looks at the counsellor. He is still quite clearly* agitated.)* I think that it's perfectly understandable that you should be feeling anxious about this return to work. *(The counsellor pauses and waits for the client to acknowledge what has been said. Eventually he nods his head slightly.)* In an ideal world, you'd be in a different office where you wouldn't be reminded all the time. *(The client nods again.)* But I'm wondering, well, so much has changed since last time. Not at work I know but in the rest of your life. So perhaps we could look at just how now is different from before. Maybe if we look at the differences rather than concentrating on what's the same, you might start to feel different.

Client: *(The client continues to nod with increasing frequency. Finally he sighs.)* Yes, yes that makes sense. Okay, then let's do that.

If you familiarise yourself with these presuppositions, have a read through and reflect a little on what they mean to you, taking note of where they might be useful, then you will have a more secure foundation for your counselling practice. It is not so much that they have to be actively thought of and recalled in counselling situations but more that you allow them to operate in the background helping you organise your thinking and communication.

8

Supportive Counselling

In this chapter, we shall explore 'Supportive Counselling' looking at what it is, how to identify when it is needed and how best to provide it. At the end of the chapter you will find a case history and transcript of a typical 'Supportive Counselling' intervention, highlighting the principles and skills described.

Although **Supportive Counselling** is considered to be the simplest form of counselling, it does none the less still require great care, thought and consideration. It is only simple relative to the more complex forms of counselling that require higher level change work. No counselling intervention should ever be taken lightly because the complexity of clients means that we can never properly predict how they might react to our help. But, with the right preparation and attention to the skills and ideas outlined in this chapter the support you offer will be greatly enhanced.

It is unlikely that anyone ever goes through life without having to face some difficulty or hardship. These are part and parcel of life and without them we would probably find it difficult to fully appreciate the better times. For many of us, difficulties are there to be overcome. We rise to the challenge they present and learn what we can. Occasionally, we may face particular difficulties that are more challenging and feel that we may be unable to cope. We may feel sad, unhappy, fearful or anxious; a whole range of 'negative' emotions that are the normal reactions to life's harder times. For most of us, most of the time these reactions are transient and with the support of friends and family, we are able to overcome the difficulties and move on to better things. There are occasions however, when despite our best efforts and the help of family and friends we still feel unable to cope and require the aid of a more objective outsider. This is the function of supportive counselling.

As a starting point, we can think of supportive counselling as a form of counselling that aims to reassure the client, supporting him or her through the process of recovery from trauma. In supportive counselling, we begin with the assumption that the client is a fundamentally healthy individual who doesn't have any specific problems that might require longer term counselling. The key concepts here are Trauma, Reassurance and Recovery and we shall explore them in more depth throughout this chapter.

Trauma

Trauma begins with an unexpected and unwanted life event but it is the individual's reaction to the event that determines the degree of traumatisation. Typically, we can assume that people have been traumatised by life events when those events have a negative affect on their normal behaviour and functioning for any length of time. This may leave them feeling sad or anxious, they may become pre-occupied with what has happened making concentration difficult, they may have difficulty sleeping or suffer other signs and symptoms of stress.

Trauma is not defined by the severity of the event but by the severity of the reaction. For example, person one might witness a quite horrific accident and yet not have a particularly strong negative reaction. He may experience little in the way of trauma. On the other hand, person two may witness something that to others might appear quite innocuous such as two friends arguing and become deeply troubled as a result. However, we are able to identify certain life events that are more likely to lead to trauma than others. These life events can be thought of as 'universals' in the sense that there is a likelihood that we might all experience them at some time in our lives either directly or through someone we know.

Some major universal life events that might lead to trauma are:

- bereavement
- injury or ill health
- redundancy
- violence or assault
- separation or divorce
- motoring accident
- burglary.

All of these have certain characteristics in common. One, they are unwanted; two, they are often unexpected; and three, they all imply some kind of change in the status quo, quite often in the form of loss or anticipated loss. It is this change that leads to the experience of trauma.

Although trauma is more likely to follow these major life events, it can and often does result from what on the surface appear to be relatively minor life events. Remember it is not the event alone that determines the degree of trauma. Other factors such as personal background, home and family life and general sense of self-esteem all play a part.

A young personnel manager was referred for counselling. She had been off sick from work for three weeks with a diagnosis of stress and anxiety. When this was explored with her it was discovered that prior to experiencing stress she had overheard two colleagues, one of them a close personal friend, talking about her in rather disparaging terms. This had caused her some initial upset but more significantly it impacted upon the friendship. She felt unable or unwilling to confront her friend and so their relationship had broken down. It was the loss of the friend that had caused the real distress.

When we are feeling good about ourselves and on top of our lives, it is hard to imagine an event like this causing such a reaction. Of course we would all be upset if this happened to us but it is unlikely that this would result in time off work. As it turned out the young lady in question had experienced more than her fair share of loss during her life. Her mother had died when she was only eight years old and a few years later her father had been killed in a motoring accident. Relationships and the permanence and security they bring were of great importance to her.

What I hope this illustrates is the importance of recognising that we are not all alike and our responses to negative life events are unique. Just because someone has not experienced a major negative life event doesn't mean they are not experiencing trauma and in our practice we need to explore all possibilities and be tolerant of the impact seemingly minor events can have. Although not exhaustive, the following are some of the minor events that might lead to trauma.

Some minor universal life events that might lead to trauma are:

- arguments or disputes
- moving away from home
- change of job status
- loss of income
- children leaving home
- birth of a child.

Kubler-Ross: the stages of bereavement

Because loss and trauma are so closely linked, it is worth looking more closely at our reaction to loss or anticipated loss. In her seminal work *'On Death and Dying'* psychologist Elizabeth Kubler-Ross explored the process of bereavement. Although, as the title indicates, this was a book primarily concerned with how we cope with death, many of the central ideas can be applied to other aspects of our lives where we experience trauma or loss.

Kubler-Ross identified five stages of bereavement following loss. She proposed that when a person loses someone or something of great importance, it takes time to recover and during this time the person will work through these five stages. Furthermore, Kubler-Ross believed these stages to be a perfectly healthy and normal response to loss.

The first stage is **Denial**. During this period the person will convince themselves that all will be well and that the loss or anticipated loss is just not happening. This denial of reality brings some peace of mind and therefore weakens the negative emotions associated with the loss. In extreme cases, there will be no conscious recognition of the facts at all and the person may become quite deluded although this is rare. More typically, they will find some way to rationalise away the loss, convincing themselves that they are all right. People in denial may on the surface appear to have adjusted to the loss quite happily.

The second stage is **Anger**. During this stage people grieving becomes increasingly angry with the perceived unfairness of their situation. It is typified by the statement 'Why me?'. They may become envious and quietly rage at others who haven't suffered such a loss, feeling cheated. Anger may also be expressed towards the object of loss.

The third stage is **Bargaining**. During the bargaining stage, grievers will try to find someone or something they can bargain with to have a 'second chance'. In the case of redundancy for example, this might be a boss.

The fourth stage is **Depression**. By this stage grievers are finally facing up to the reality of the situation and feeling the full force of their sadness at the loss. It is the stage most usually associated with the grieving process. Often the person will be outwardly emotional during this stage but it is normally recognised as the first sign that the person is overcoming his or her loss.

The fifth and final stage is **Acceptance**. Grievers finally come to fully accept the reality of their loss and are able to move on in life. Often they will make their peace with the object of loss and clear up any 'unfinished business'.

Kubler-Ross's stages are a useful tool in helping us understand the process of grieving but ever since they were first published, they have come under criticism. The critics argue that not everyone necessarily goes through all the stages. The health professional or counsellor working with the bereaved may unwittingly try to force the model onto the client. But, this is not really a fair criticism of the model itself, it is more a criticism of how the model is often applied and that kind of criticism can be aimed at any theory or model.

Another criticism of this model is that in reality recovery from trauma or loss rarely goes smoothly. It is unlikely that an individual will go through each of the stages in order with equal ease. Much more likely is oscillation between the various stages with an overall move towards acceptance.

Ideal Path of Recovery

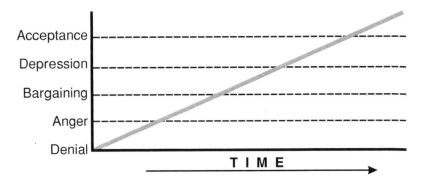

More Realistic Path of Recovery

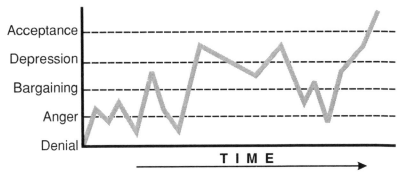

Figure 10

Satir categories

Individual difference also plays a large part in determining how we react to loss or trauma. In the 1960s, family therapist Virginia Satir put forward a model which categorises preferred styles for coping with distress. These have become widely adopted in many schools of psychotherapy and are known as the 'Satir Categories'. What Satir noticed through her many hours of working with families was that, as individuals, we each respond to pressure differently but that these differences could be matched with four overall coping styles or categories.

The first Satir Category is **Distracter**. According to Satir, many people attempt to cope with pressure or stress by distracting themselves and others with flighty and often irrelevant behaviour. The Distracter will jump from one topic of conversation to another in an often manic and chaotic way. Non-verbally, they will appear fidgety and uncoordinated. The Distracter will often appear humourous or even flirtatious and can be fun if somewhat wearing to be around. In many ways, the Distracter is similar to a person working through the denial stage of the Kubler-Ross model.

Satir called her second category **Blamer**. The Blamer will cope with distress by looking outwardly for people or objects to blame. There is often much anger connected with Blamers' behaviour and their language is accusatory and hostile. Non-verbally, there is much pointing and finger wagging. Obviously the Blamer is closely linked with the Kubler-Ross stage of anger.

Satir's third category is **Placator**. The Placator will take full responsibility for the distressing situation in an attempt to diffuse any anger or hostility from others. For Placators, everything is ultimately their fault and they often feel full of guilt and remorse. They just want everyone to feel happy and will take on all the world's troubles in an attempt to achieve this. The Placator does not really correspond with any of the Kubler-Ross stages although placatory behaviour can often be seen during the bargaining and depression stages.

The final Satir Category is **Super-Reasonable** or **Computer**. The computer attempts to rise above it all in an effort to cope with distress.

Being a computer is all about being grown up and sensible. If everyone can just be reasonable about the situation, then all will be well. There is little emotion associated with this category. The Computer is above 'irrational' emotions. Again this category does not fit neatly with the Kubler-Ross model although elements of this type of behaviour may be found in the denial, bargaining and acceptance stages. It is important to note that Computers will often give the impression that they have a reasonable perspective on everything and have reached the stage of acceptance when in reality they may still be working through any of the other stages. How they appear to others is often more important than how they feel inside.

When recovery from trauma is explored making use of the Satir Categories, it becomes easy to see how these individual differences might impact upon the sufferer and it is therefore useful to keep these in mind when offering supportive counselling.

Although the Kubler-Ross model is useful in tracking the progress a person is making in recovering from loss it is less useful for explaining the underlying process of recovery. In recent years, we have been able to model the process more usefully through our experience in counselling many individuals who have been traumatised in some way or another. This has resulted in the development of a three-stage model that explains some of the underlying processes of recovery.

The three-stage coping model

Stage 1: Trauma coping

Stage one is the trauma itself. During this stage, the client will be extremely pre-occupied with the negative events that led to the trauma and there is likely to be considerable emotional upset. Conversely, an emotional 'numbness' to the events may be experienced if the emotions are overwhelming. It would appear that unconsciously we are able to 'shut down' our emotions if they cross a certain threshold of intensity. This is simply a coping mechanism and it is likely that after a while, the negative emotions will once more surface. There is typically a considerable feeling of helplessness and associated anxiety. Clients are unable to control their thoughts and feel they are out of control of their fear. In this stage, clients are often extremely self focused often unable to think of anyone or anything other than themselves and their current distress. They are almost universally past-orientated, continually reliving the events that led to the trauma. The present and future are beyond their concerns. As they relive the events they are typically fully associated within the memory, literally 'reliving' as if they were there again. Often this reliving comes unbidden in the form of flashbacks which seem to occur more frequently at night. The submodalities of the memories are usually vivid, large, colourful and loud with quite extreme submodality distortion taking place. The thinking and reasoning about the events is usually circular with all thoughts about the events leading back to the same starting point. In talking with others, the client is likely to continually recount the events in increasing amounts of detail. This way of responding seems to serve the useful function of helping ensure that the client takes necessary learnings from the bad experience. Obviously, the greater the threat to the client the more important it is that he or she learns from the experience and so circular thinking and continually reliving the experience maximise the chances of learning taking place.

Stage 2: Fantasy coping

As the immediate strength of negative emotions starts to diminish (and this could take anything from a few hours to several weeks) the clients enters a stage that we call **Fantasy Coping**. This is typified by the desire to change the past in some way. The client will often relive the traumatic experience, unconsciously changing the events to have them turn out in a more desirable way. There will often be considerable anger and bitterness expressed during this stage with statements like 'Why me?' And 'If only…' frequently cropping up in conversation. It would seem that this stage functions to aid learning having the client recreate different possible scenarios, responses and outcomes. We shall see an example of this highlighted in the case history transcript at the end of this chapter. During this stage, the client becomes decreasingly pre-occupied with the events that led to the trauma and, as the re-living of the experience changes and diminishes there is an increase in the client's 'thinking about' the experience in a more abstract way. The experience is becoming increasingly interpreted in the search for new meaning and new understanding. Clients are likely to become less self-focused and more focused on others and the world at large perhaps looking for reasons for their distress that lie beyond themselves. When recalling the experience that led to the trauma, clients are likely to become increasingly dissociated from their memory as if watching it happen to someone else. This distancing serves the very useful function of decreasing the intensity of negative emotions associated with the experience. It also becomes increasingly easy for clients to be distracted from their remembering of the traumatic event. There is still a tendency for clients to be past-orientated but, as time passes, they become increasingly attentive to the present and the future.

Stage 3: Reality coping

Eventually clients begin to gain a healthier and more realistic perspective on the events that led to trauma; they learn to cope with the reality of the situation. This is a process of acceptance of the facts and all that they imply. There is a growing desire to learn from the experience and move on. Attention shifts from being past-orientated to becoming increasingly focused on the present and the future. When recalling the events that led to trauma, clients are now fully dissociated and their thinking about the events is more abstract. By this stage, their thinking is no longer circular and they have regained full control over its direction. By the time clients reach this point, we can assume that they have fully recovered from the trauma.

Cognition in the Three-stage Coping Model

	Attention 1	Attention 2	Submodalities	Abstraction	Thinking
Trauma coping	Self-focused	Past	Associated Vivid Loud	Concrete Sensory Specific	Circular
Fantasy coping	Other/ World focused	Past ↓ Present Future	Associated ↓ Dissociated	Concrete ↓ Abstract	Circular ↓ Linear
Reality coping	Self-other World Balanced	Present Future	Dissociated Less intense Quieter	Abstract	Linear

Figure 11

To some extent the splitting of this process into three stages is arbitrary and so focussing on them as content distinctions is not so useful. It is more important to understand and appreciate the underlying process of recovery and the important function this process serves. The central organising theme of the process of recovery from trauma seems to be learning and the need to learn. Whilst at a conscious level we may simply desire to no longer feel bad, at a more unconscious level the need to learn from the experience and so avoid a repeat is very strong. This basic survival mechanism drives the preoccupation, constant reliving of events and flashbacks that typify the trauma stage. Unconsciously, we attempt to extract every last piece of learning we can from the experience and will not move on to later stages until we have. Understanding the importance of this and the very positive function it serves is essential when offering supportive counselling to trauma sufferers. Indeed, one of the main ways in which people can become 'stuck' in the early stages of recovery is by fighting this process. Of course, the client has no desire to feel emotionally upset and so understandably attempts to suppress or control their out-of-control thoughts, often by resorting to the use of alcohol or prescription tranquillisers. Whilst there is obviously a place for such relief from traumatising memories, helping the client understand and appreciate their positive function will ultimately lead to a speedier recovery.

Reassurance

As we said at the beginning of this chapter the main function of supportive counselling is to offer reassurance and so it is going to be worthwhile to spend some time exploring how this can be most effectively offered.

In all likelihood, you will have found yourself in a situation at some time in your life when you have been upset or worried and confided in a friend or colleague. They probably listened carefully to you and then said everything they could to reassure you that it was all going to be all right. Did their reassurances convince you at the time? Probably not because at the time you were upset, concerned and preoccupied with your worries and, kind though their words were, from your perspective then, they were less than convincing. We call this type of reassurance **direct reassurance**, deliberately and consciously reassuring someone that all will be well, and it seems the natural thing to offer when we are trying to support a friend or colleague. However, it is problematic and here is why.

Firstly, when a person is traumatised and preoccupied with traumatic memories, they have a great need to explore all the negative implications of what has happened. Remember what was said earlier about learning. At this time they will be very negatively orientated, searching for all the things that could possibly go wrong as a result of what has happened. From within this mind-set, words of reassurance are more likely to be met with what is known as a **polarity response**. You may offer, 'You'll be all right,' as a well intentioned reassurance, but the polarity response to this is, 'No, I won't'. There is a strong probability that they will then search for reasons to justify the belief that they won't be all right and, the more you try to reassure the more reasons they will find for why they won't.

Secondly, direct reassurance can simply confirm and reinforce the concerns of the client. If there really isn't anything to be concerned about, then why are they being reassured. You may offer, 'You'll be all right,' and they may respond with, 'I know I will,' but, privately they may well be thinking that you must be worried that they won't – otherwise why reassure?

Finally, direct reassurance can set up unrealistic expectations. How can we ever be really sure that the client will be all right? Sadly, there will be occasions when it is all too obvious that the client's outlook is not good and reassurances are at best hollow words and at worst they create false hope.

More useful as meaningful reassurance is indirect reassurance which comes about when the counsellor fully believes that the client will be able to make the best of circumstances. If, as a counsellor, you are able to adopt the attitude that, together with the client, you will be able to make a difference and that they will feel better about circumstances as a result of your help, then unconsciously you will communicate this to the client. They will pick up on your confidence in them through unconscious communication such as body language and voice tone. You are not joining them in their distress because you fully appreciate that it is not a permanent state of affairs. Of course, you do sympathise with their plight and you care about the fact that they are distressed but, unlike the client, you are not overwhelmed by it.

Indirect reassurance is about keeping a wider perspective, seeing clients as whole people and not just as people currently in distress. Your care is shown by your interest in their story and the more you are able to convey your appreciation of the richness of their experiences, the more you will communicate your caring. Remember that the process for them is one of learning and it is this that you need to show most concern for. This in itself is greatly reassuring. Clients realise that, no matter how bad they feel, you are not overwhelmed by their stories. Quite the opposite, you are intrigued by their stories and want to help them learn from what has happened so that they are able to recover and move on.

Keep in mind that the clients are going through a period which to them probably feels a little unreal. It isn't 'normal' for them to feel this way. You can offer considerable reassurance by helping them 'normalise' their experience and this is achieved by feeling comfortable talking about things other than their current distress. In particular, talk about positive, future events such as holidays. By doing this, you are pre-supposing that recovery will happen and at the same time re-enforcing a wider, healthier perspective.

Finally, it is important to remain grounded in reality. Do not avoid hard issues. If there are particularly painful aspects to the clients' experiences, avoidance of these issue can lead to a magnification of their impact. The longer you avoid talking about them, the more important they become. Helping clients face the reality of their situation will ultimately help them move on and recover because to maximise learning they need to explore the totality of their experiences. Above all, avoid getting drawn into any unrealistic fantasies. Yes, these will offer some immediate relief but they only prolong the proper process of recovery. Although obvious, it is worth remembering that we cannot change the past. What has happened has happened and no amount of wishing it otherwise will change that. What can be influenced is how the past is reacted to.

Recovery

Reassurance is the means by which we help someone on the road to recovery but it is also important to track this process and remain alert to any signs that the client has become 'stuck' at some stage in the process.

Unfortunately, this is not as easy as it would seem. Because of differences in both the clients and their circumstances, it is impossible to say how long the process of recovery should take. For some in might be a matter of hours, for others it could be months.

The only practical way of tracking clients' progress is to notice changes in both their outward behaviour and in their reports of their subjective experience. This can be done by making full use of the three stage model outlined above, noticing changes both within and between counselling sessions. As long as there is change, then it is safe to assume that the clients are making progress even if they are not necessarily feeling any better. The ultimate goal is for them to feel better but there are times during the process of recovery when they might, in the short term, feel worse, and it is important to appreciate this. As a general rule of thumb, if there has been no change across three or more sessions of counselling, then err on the side of caution and consider referring the client on to a more qualified counsellor. It may be that the client is simply slow to recover but equally this could indicate a deeper problem that requires more help than you are qualified to offer.

Case history and session transcript

This client's name is Dan. He is a forty-one year old man working as an engineer in a large manufacturing plant. He has worked for the company for twenty years and has a good work record. He is hardworking and conscientious and popular with his work colleagues. Dan is a happily married man with two teenage daughters. He is in good physical health and has no history of any mental health problems.

Recently Dan was supervising the removal of a heavy piece of machinery for routine maintenance. This was a routine if somewhat tricky job he had performed many times before. Three junior staff were helping Dan in this task. Everything seemed to be going smoothly when a supporting strap slipped as the machinery was being winched up. Before any one could react, the machinery tipped up and fell to the shop floor with an alarming crash. Luckily no one was beneath it at the time or they would have been severely injured if not killed. As it was, considerable damage was done to both the machinery and the surrounding area.

Dan was severely shaken by the incident and the following day was sent home when it was clear that he was not able to perform his duties. A few weeks later and still very distressed, Dan was referred for counselling.

The following transcript is taken from the first session of counselling. Notes are provided in order to highlight key points.

Session One

(This section of transcript is taken after the formal introductions and other issues normally discussed at the commencement of counselling. The counsellor has been provided with some information regarding the client's case.)

Counsellor: So Dan, it's over to you. Where would you like to begin?

Dan: Well, you know what happened right? *(Counsellor nods)* Okay, well, I'm not sure ... I don't know why, but ever since, I've felt terrible – it's like I just can't stop thinking about it ... all the time. I can't get anything done – it's just there all the time. *(Dan's voice is quite tremulous as he recounts this and he is fidgeting, appearing to be in some discomfort)*

Counsellor: What ... that's like the memory of what happened?

Dan: Yeah just seeing it falling and the noise ... it's worse at night – it keeps waking me up, the noise of it falling and I'm like shaking all over.

Counsellor: And, have you been able to talk to anyone about this? I mean before now.

Dan: Well, there's the wife but she doesn't really know what to do to help. She just keeps saying it wasn't anyone's fault so I shouldn't worry about it.

Counsellor: Is she right? Was it anyone's fault? *(The counsellor is not avoiding a difficult question. It is important to establish responsibility from the outset.)*

Dan: Well, that's the problem, really. I don't know. I keep thinking it over and really we did everything we should have done but then I think maybe there was a something else.

Counsellor: But you've done this sort of job before?

Dan: Oh, yeah, loads of times.

Counsellor: And you've never had a problem like this?

Dan: No, it's always gone really smoothly. Well, we have this procedure ... like a safety procedure we have to follow.

Counsellor: And you followed the procedure, right?

Dan: Oh yeah. Yeah, I always pride myself in working to procedure. It's just that the procedure ... well it's complicated but basically it doesn't cover for what happened. No one really knows how it happened.

Counsellor: So if you were in the same situation again it could happen again?

Dan: Well no not really because now I'd make sure I checked the balance... that's not in the procedure. Maybe we need to change the procedure now.

Counsellor: Okay, I see. So you followed the procedure but it didn't cover what happened but now you'd do things differently and it wouldn't happen again.

Dan: Yeah, although I keep thinking, why didn't I check the balance anyway?

Counsellor: Because it's not in the procedure?

Dan: Yeah, but the procedures can't cover everything.

Counsellor: Well, let me think about this for a minute. It seems to me that you have this procedure to help ensure safety and that you followed the procedure. And, probably there was a time when jobs like this were performed without any safety procedure at all right? *(Dan nods his head)* And then probably there were one or two incidents and someone came up with the bright idea of introducing a safety procedure. And, over time, as other things went wrong, that procedure grew. They learned from mistakes that were made.

Dan: Yeah something like that I suppose. I actually helped write this particular procedure a couple of years ago ... the old one was a bit confusing.

Counsellor: *(Here we can see how the counsellor is deliberately placing the client's experience into a wider historical, learning perspective, by referring to the development of the procedure over time and of how it was developed on the basis of experience.)* So now, what? The procedure will be rewritten again as a result of what happened?

Dan: Well, yeah, I suppose so ... probably not the whole thing – it'll just be added to.

Counsellor: Okay, well that's a good thing I guess.

Dan: Makes you wonder though, doesn't it?

Counsellor:	Sorry, I'm not sure I'm with you.
Dan:	Well if this could happen, what else could happen. Things we haven't thought of. *(This is very typical thinking on the part of a trauma sufferer. In a desperate attempt to avoid a similar incident in the future there is an over-compensation – and attempts to cover every possible future.)*
Counsellor:	Well, yes, I suppose there are other possibilities but we can never anticipate every possibility – that would be impossible.
Dan:	Yeah, I know you're right – it's just I can't stop these thoughts. It's doing my head in.
Counsellor:	Okay, well, suppose I told you that what you're going through is a perfectly normal reaction to a very unusual and frightening experience.
Dan:	Well, I've been through shit before and I've never felt like this.
Counsellor:	Okay, do you think that there is something else wrong here? Have you ever felt this way before at any time?
Dan:	No, no … I know it's to do with the accident. I just wish I could forget it all and get on with things. But then…someone could have been killed you know?
Counsellor:	Yeah, and that's a frightening thought. People do get killed in accidents and it's usually nobody's fault. I guess we just find it hard to accept that. *(Again the counsellor is offering a wider and more realistic perspective. There is a long silence at this point and the client appears very pre-occupied.)*
Dan:	So what do I do? How can I stop feeling so shit and get all of this out of my head?
Counsellor:	Well, it's a funny thing the human mind…
Dan:	*(Grinning)* You can say that again.
Counsellor:	But really, why do you think it keeps bringing up all these memories of the accident?
Dan:	I don't know … really I don't – I just want to forget it … like have it so it never happened
Counsellor:	What if that isn't possible?
Dan:	Well, Christ, I can't go on like this.
Counsellor:	No, not like this but, if you forgot it completely, then you'd never know to check the balance in future would you? *(The*

counsellor returns to the learning perspective set up earlier.)

Dan: No, I suppose not.

Counsellor: And, next time there might be someone underneath when it falls.

Dan: Oh God, I keep seeing that too. What if there had been someone underneath?... and it's such a relief there wasn't. *(This indicates clearly that the client is employing fantasy coping.)*

Counsellor: Okay, this is really important. You've been having all these flashbacks and unwanted thoughts and you've been feeling really bad since this happened but, in that time, have the thoughts or feelings changed in any way? Have there been any differences in their content or the quality of them in any way.

Dan: I'm not sure what you mean ... after it first happened I was just numb and then the flashbacks started. I suppose it's only in the last week that I've really been able to think about it properly so I guess it has changed yeah.

Counsellor: And, it will carry on changing. That's how the mind works. The feelings ... the bad feelings will diminish and you'll find yourself thinking less and less about it as time goes on. When you're ready, you'll be able to put it properly in place. *(Although this is quite a direct piece of reassurance, the counsellor can be confident that the process of recovery is well under way based on what was said previously. The counsellor delivers this with considerable congruence and certainty which adds weight to the reassurance.)*

Dan: Well, I hope you're right.

Counsellor: So, are you going to be working on the new procedure when you're back at work? *(The counsellor is presupposing a full recovery.)*

Dan: I'm not sure, I need to see Derek – he's the safety officer. They're still waiting for the final report.

Counsellor: Well, it's a good job they have someone like you to help with it. You obviously take your work very seriously.

Dan: (The client shrugs.) So in the mean time what should I do

	about the flashbacks? They're worse at night ... I really am finding it very difficult.
Counsellor:	I think at this stage we just need to let them run their course. I can't think of any reason why they should go on much longer. Pay attention to how they change over time and start to explore not 'if you have any control over them,' but 'what control can you exert over them.'
Dan:	Sorry, I don't understand.
Counsellor:	Well, when you daydream or imagine things normally, you've probably noticed that you can change your thoughts quite deliberately. You know, if you imagine going on holiday and in your mind's eye you change the place where you are going ... that sort of thing.
Dan:	Yeah, I get that.
Counsellor:	Okay then, when the flashbacks come, try to step back a little and see what you can influence about the memory. Might not be much at first but, over time, you might be surprised at just how you can alter them. *(The counsellor is presupposing that the client will regain control over his thoughts and suggested how this might come about. This at least gives the client some direction.)*
Dan:	Okay I'll give that a go. You think it will help?
Counsellor:	Probably not straight away no. But, give it time and you'll find that you can increasingly get control back over your thoughts. And, I'll see you again next week some time, to see how you're progressing.

Notice that the counsellor is not leaving the client set up with any unrealistic expectations. It's been made clear that the process of recovery will take some time but, it has also been made clear, both directly and indirectly through pre-supposition, that the client will make a full recovery.

A key moment in this session was the counsellor's identification that the client's thought processes had changed through time. The counsellor uses this, together with other pieces of information such as the fact that the client has no previous history of 'out of control' thoughts to assess the level of counselling required. If for example the client had answered that there had been no change whatsoever in the thoughts and 'flash backs' he had experienced since the incident, then the counsellor would need to explore the possibility that a more involved level of problem solving or therapeutic counselling might be required. However, because the thoughts had changed through time and, because the client gave a clear example of having moved into a fantasy coping stage, the counsellor can feel confident that it is supportive counselling that is required.

Consider also the potential scenario had the counsellor assessed the counselling needs inaccurately. If the counsellor had decided that the client had a serious problem that required more involved counselling, there is the very real danger of prolonging the suffering. The client is recovering – this is what was important – and the counsellor's role in this situation is to offer support and useful reassurance.

In conclusion, when offering supportive counselling, always work well within your comfort zone. If you are at all fazed or distressed by your client's story or are unsure about your ability to help then you can be certain that your client will pick up on this thereby undermining any attempts to help. If in doubt, refer on.

9

Problem-solving Counselling

The majority of people who seek out counselling do so because they face some problem or collection of problems for which they can find no solution. Sometimes, on further investigation, it becomes apparent that the problems they face are examples of a more universal and deep-seated issue for which they require a therapeutic intervention but, more often than not there are no underlying issues, they are simply struggling with their current circumstances. We have already talked a little about the difference between problem-solving counselling and therapeutic counselling in an earlier chapter and we shall have more to say about this difference in the next chapter. In this chapter, I want to focus on how to help the client who presents with a specific difficulty or problem.

As with supportive counselling, we begin with the assumption that the client is an otherwise healthy individual with no history of mental health problems or other psychological difficulties. It is also fair to assume that clients are seeking help through counselling only after having tried everything within their know-how and abilities to resolve the problem themselves.

Problem-solving counselling is not about you the counsellor finding answers to the problems but rather about you the counsellor *helping the client* find solutions to the problems. Typically, clients rarely act on the direct advice or suggestions of others irrespective of the quality of the advice. They are much more likely to resolve the problem when they have found the solution themselves.

A well-formed problem

Before we explore some of the models and approaches that can be used in problem solving counselling, it is important to first clarify what we mean when we talk about a problem. Although this may seem a straightforward enough task, it is only when we begin to explore a client's understanding that we begin to realise just how difficult it can be to pin down exactly what the problem is.

Perhaps surprisingly, the first challenge is often in establishing a specific problem that can be realistically influenced through counselling. Clients are often reluctant to accept that a problem might lie within them and instead project the problem out into the world and current circumstances. When asked what the problem is they will often go to great lengths in describing a set of difficult external circumstances with little or no reference to themselves and how they are failing to cope with those circumstances. Take the following example.

A thirty-four year old engineering manager came into counselling explaining that he was finding it hard to concentrate on his work. On investigation, he described that the problem started when he was asked to share his office with two other managers. Previously, he had an office to himself. When pressed he was adamant that the problem was with his managers who had insisted on the office sharing. Now, one solution to the problem might have been for him to persuade his managers that he needed his own office and it may be that counselling could have helped him plan how to achieve this but he was adamant that management would not be influenced on this issue.

The counsellor is now faced with a problem. What can be done to offer any effective help? One possibility would be to re-think the problem and tackle it through supportive counselling; helping the client come to terms with the change in circumstances. A second possibility would be to back the client up through questioning until he is able to identify something within how he is trying to deal with the circumstances that is problematic. Then a problem-solving approach could be utilised, but until this is achieved there is no client-centred problem to be worked on. To continue with the above example, a supportive counselling approach might eventually lead to the client accepting that the new arrangements will make it hard for him to be as productive as he once was. A problem-solving approach on the other hand might help the client recognise that it is because of the way he is thinking about the new circumstances that he is experiencing problems or that he is not yet used to working with others and that he simply needs time and practice to adjust. The important issue here is that as problem-solving counsellors, we can only directly influence clients and how they are coping with their life circumstances – we cannot directly influence the life circumstances.

A simple way to decide whether a stated problem is client-centred or circumstance-centred is to ask ourselves the question:

'Is it the case that for everyone and anyone finding themselves in this client's unique circumstances there would be a problem similar to the clients?'

If the answer to this is yes – that these circumstances would always be problematic no matter who experienced them – then we can safely assume that the problem is circumstance-centred and we could consider either helping the client change the circumstances or if they can't be changed, helping the client come to terms with the circumstances through supportive counselling. A good example of this would be in the case of redundancy. It is highly likely that for just about anybody who found themselves in the situation where they were being made redundant, it would be problematic. This would be a circumstance-centred problem.

If, on the other hand, the answer to the above question was no, then we would need to help the client identify what it was about how they were dealing with the circumstances that was problematic; we help them identify a client-centred problem. The following flow chart details the steps in this process.

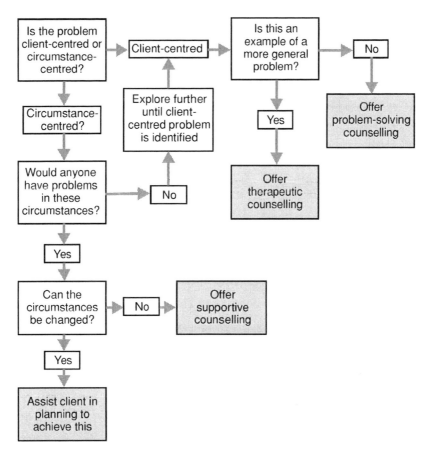

Figure 12

Problem-solving planner

Once a well-formed problem that can be resolved with the help of problem-solving counselling has been identified, it may be tempting to begin to explore possible solutions but this would be premature. Identifying the problem is only the first part of building a full and useful understanding of the problem; an understanding that will be essential if a permanent, effective and ecological solution is to be found.

The problem-solving planner is a relatively straightforward model that provides a framework for problem exploration.

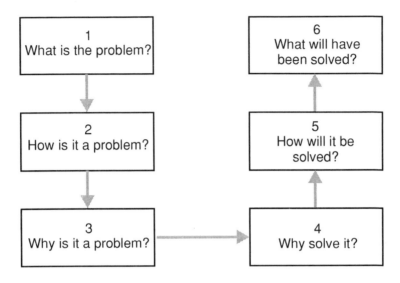

Figure 13

Although each step is identified by a specific question, rather than think of these as questions requiring single answers it is more useful to think of them as general headings for further exploration. The counsellor should make full use of their information gathering skills developed in earlier chapters in building a thorough understanding of the clients answers in each of the steps.

In general terms, when exploring the left hand column of the planner, the client will be 'negatively orientated', focussing on the problem he or she is trying to solve. Working up the right hand column of the planner shifts the focus of attention towards the more positive orientation of the solution. Working through the planner in this way helps set a useful directional pattern so that even though the first and last question may appear on first viewing to be very similar, because of the very different orientation, the answers are likely to be quite different.

Of all of the steps in the planner, the first and last are usually the most straightforward in that they require a fairly descriptive answer. 'What' questions are generally easier to answer than 'How' and 'Why' questions. The aim of asking the 'How' questions is to try and establish the full scope of the workings and mechanics of the problem and possible solutions. Included in this should be explanations of the client's beliefs and values relating to the problem and not just a more complex description of the circumstances.

The 'Why' questions allow for the most variability in types of answer. At one level, the client could answer in terms of why the circumstances are problematic in the first place, whilst on another level they could answer in terms of why the problem manifests in the way it does. All types of answer to the 'Why' question's are worth exploring.

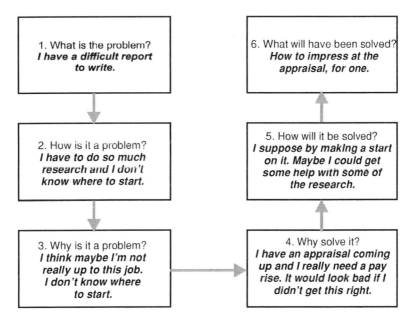

Figure 14

The problem is the solution

Great care should be taken when helping clients explore and identify possible solutions to their problems. In an earlier chapter, mention was made of the work of Paul Watzlawick and his colleagues from the Paulo Alto Mental Research Institute. Watzlawick demonstrated how attempts at solutions can often exacerbate the original problem. This is most likely to happen if the problem is not properly understood and the solution not well formed. Watzlawick et al identified three ways in which this could happen and more recently McWhirter added a fourth. These are:

1. **Action is necessary but not taken.** The client attempts to solve the problem by ignoring it in the hope that it will go away. This usually happens when the client is overwhelmed by the problem finding it difficult to know how to react. The client 'buries his heads in the sand' in the hope that the problem will go away.

   A young woman came to counselling on the recommendation of her manager who was becoming increasingly concerned about the woman's attendance record. It turned out that the woman was having quite serious marital problems; her husband had been having an affair with a close friend for several months. The client was attempting to deal with this unhappy scenario by pretending everything was okay and hoping that, given time, her husband would see sense and put a stop to the affair. Eventually, as a result of counselling, she was able to confront her husband and take some control of the situation.

2. **Action is taken when it shouldn't be.** Some situations appear more problematic than they really are. A good example of this is the bereavement process described in the last chapter. As was stated there, this process is a natural and healthy response to trauma that, left to run its course, ultimately leads to acceptance and adaptation. But, of course many of the negative emotions experienced during this process are unpleasant, leading to the mistaken belief that the emotions themselves are a problem to be got rid of. Action is taken to suppress or replace the negative

emotions, through the use of medication or alcohol for example, and if these don't work, clients can come to believe that there is something wrong with them, that they shouldn't feel the way they do. Not only can this interfere with a very natural and healthy process, it can also create for the clients mistaken beliefs about their mental health and well-being.

3. **Action is taken at the wrong level.**

A new factory manager saw that there was a problem with inter-departmental communication. His solution was to send all of the heads of department on assertiveness training workshops. This was not only hugely time consuming and expensive, it was also totally unnecessary. The problem was simply one of protocol and eventually it was realised that a simple reorganisation of interdepartmental meeting schedules would solve the problem. In the meantime, many of the departmental managers had become resentful at the implications of sending them on the course. This is a classic example of a solution mismatching a problem in terms of level.

The manager's solution was pitched at a higher level than was necessary to resolve the problem. At other times a solution may be attempted at too low a level for the problem. In these situations the client may be guilty of 'over simplification', for example in the case of the employee who takes an unscheduled holiday as a solution to the growing stress and pressure of work rather than tackling the causes of the stress more directly.

4. **Action is taken in the wrong area.** This occurs when a problem manifests in one area of the client's life, for example at work, and the client attempts to solve the problem by addressing the issue in a different area of their lives such as home. Again this usually comes about as the result of poor understanding of the problem. The manager who buries himself in work pushing himself to ever greater achievements when his home and family life are falling apart is a classic example of this pattern.

Well-formed outcomes

Once the problem has been thoroughly explored using the problem-solving planner, it is time to turn our attention to the future and help our clients identify more clearly what kind of a result they want from their solutions.

In the 1970s, the early pioneers of NLP created a procedure for creating **Well-formed Outcomes**. They based this procedure on the modelling of high achievers and identified a list of conditions that maximised the likelihood that an outcome would be achieved. Up until this time the major focus in most forms of therapy and change work had been on understanding and working with the problem state. Few people considered the importance of having a clearer picture of what was desired for the future.

When clients come to us for help, it is highly likely that they will be most aware of the negative events and feelings they are experiencing making it hard for them to consider what they do want to experience instead; their preoccupation is with getting rid of the unwanted problem. The well-formed outcome procedure shifts the emphasis and helps clarify desirable 'moving towards' motivation. The benefits of this are manifold. Paramount is the fact that when we are so aware of what we *don't* want, but unclear of what we *do* want there will be a tendency to move towards anything that is better than the current state, irrespective of the wider implications.

Consider a person trapped in a room that is on fire, in his haste to get away from the danger of the burning room, he leaps from the window realising too late that it is on the tenth floor. More relevant, consider the amount of people who turn to alcohol or other drugs in times of stress; anything will do as long as it gets rid of the bad feelings. By having a clearer view of desired outcomes, many of the overly simplistic or overly complicated solutions mentioned previously can be avoided.

The well-formed outcome procedure has been refined and updated over the years. The version used here is widely utilised and has proven highly effective in helping resolve problems. The procedure lists six steps or conditions that need to be checked and explored in order to ensure that an outcome is well-formed. For each of these, I have included a simple example of planning for a holiday. I have also listed some of the questions that can be asked for each of the conditions.

The well-formed outcomes conditions

1. State outcome positively

Often when asked what they want, clients will describe what it is they don't want or what they want to be rid of. This condition is about checking and if necessary re-structuring the outcome to ensure it describes what is wanted in a positive sense. This makes it considerably easier to aim for something specific. Without a positively stated outcome there is a high probability that a client will remain stuck with a problem.

Holiday example: Easier for a travel agent to determine where you want to go rather than where you don't want to go.
Example questions: What do you want? – use information gathering questions from the language model throughout.

2. Outcome level and direction

Is the outcome appropriate to the problem? And, does it fit comfortably with other directions? To be successful, it is best if individual outcomes can be linked to higher-level directions and this condition helps achieve that.

Holiday example: Is the holiday a means to achieve a higher-level outcome. For example – cope with job better – relax – get away.
Example questions: What will that do for you? What are the benefits? Do you still want to go for the original outcome?

3. Evidence

Is the client able to imagine a full sensory-based representation of the outcome? Establishing what they will see, hear and feel when they have achieved the outcome. This makes the outcome more tangible and helps increase motivation as well as providing a good check so that the client knows when they have achieved the outcome. Strange as it may seem, it is not at all uncommon for people to continue to strive for an outcome long after they have achieved it because they hadn't realised they had already achieved it.

Holiday example: Direct experience, snapshots, souvenirs etc
Example questions: How will you know? How will I know? How will others know?

4. Appropriately contextualised

Ensuring that the time and place for the achievement of the outcome is appropriate. Sometimes clients want certain changes but fail to think about the appropriateness. A client who becomes more assertive and then finds he is without friends is a classic example. Being assertive at work was appropriate for this client but, because he hadn't contextualised the change, he was being overly assertive with friends, family and in social situations.

Holiday example: When and where to go. When and where not to go. How long to go for.
Example questions: When and where do you want it? When and where don't you want it? How long for?

5. Initiated and maintained by client

Ensuring that the outcome is realistic in terms of the client's resources and ability to influence the outcome. Sometimes clients ask for things that are way beyond their control. This is simply fantasy and unworkable as an outcome. The client must be in the driving seat and any external influences that might affect the achievement of the outcome need to be considered.

Holiday example: Time off work, passport, money ticket etc.
Example questions: What do you need? What stops you?

6. Ecology

Ensuring that the outcome adds choice and does not take choice away – the wider implications of achieving the outcome, especially any possible negative side effects. Sometimes clients aim for outcomes that although effective for short-term problem relief may cause even more problems in the long run. The ecology check is concerned with safeguarding against negative, wider implications of change. Checking the ecology should never just be about what the clients think – they will often not be in a position to really consider wider implications. Therefore as a counsellor it is your responsibility to help them identify these.

Holiday example: Effect on rest of life. What will you gain? – fun, relaxation. What will you lose? – money etc.
Holiday example: How will this effect the rest of your life? What might you you gain? What might you lose? Is it worthwhile?

By the time clients have been taken through this process, they will have formed an increased understanding of their problems, arrived at some possible solutions and formed a realistic and worthwhile outcome. Remember, the job of the counsellor is not to find solutions for the clients but rather to help them explore their problems in such a way as to maximise the chance of their finding an appropriate and lasting solution.

Case history and session transcript
This transcript is taken from an early session with a middle age personnel manager. The client had been suffering from numerous tension-related headaches, she had been snappy and bad tempered

with work colleagues and her marriage of twelve years was suffering, with her husband threatening to leave her. Historically, she was always ambitious and hardworking, often staying on late at work to complete deadlines. She was referred to counselling following a visit to the occupational health doctor during which she broke down in tears saying she couldn't cope any more. On her first visit, the client was reticent about discussing her circumstances stating that counselling wasn't really necessary. She seemed mildly ashamed of what had happened during her occupational health visit.

Session 3

During the first two sessions, some degree of rapport was established but little in the way of concrete exploration of the client's circumstances had taken place. However, towards the end of the second session, the client did begin to relax and entertain the possibility that counselling might be useful. She arrived for session three in a very much more open frame of mind and opened the session with a positive statement about a change she felt was needed in her life. In this session, the counsellor makes use of the **well-formed outcome** procedure to help the client arrive at a workable outcome. Note also that the language model is used throughout to help the client flesh out the detail and make the outcome more realistically achievable.

Client:	Right, well, I've been giving this a lot of thought over the past week and I think I know what I need to do.
Counsellor:	Mmm ... sounds promising.
Client:	It's pretty obvious really, but I don't know, I probably didn't want to see it this way. Anyway, what I want – what I need – is to start spending more time with my family. I just spend far too much time wrapped up in work. I need to be with my family more, doing things with them.
Counsellor:	Okay, you mean just like finishing work earlier, that sort of thing?
Client:	Yes. That makes it sound so easy doesn't it *(smiles)* as if I haven't got enough on my plate – I hardly get enough time as

it is.

Counsellor: Well, there's only twenty-four hours in a day and that's a constant. There's nothing we can do to change that one but, even though right now you feel you have too much to do at work, you know you want to spend more time with your family.

Client: I don't know if I want to but if I don't, then Dave is going to leave me – I understand that. I have to spend more time with them – it's as simple as that.

Counsellor: Just more time?

Client: Yes, just more time. *(long pause)* Well, no, not just more time, not really. I need to be more with them if that makes sense. Usually my head is so full of important stuff from work that I spend most of my time thinking about that.

Counsellor: So, it's how you are when you are with them as well. It sounds like it's not just more time but more attention you need. Maybe even the same amount of time as now will do if you were able to attend more.

Client: Maybe, I'm not sure. I think if I gave more time, I'd have more time to switch off from work, you know, and get into family stuff.

Counsellor: So you need time to make that transition?

Client: Yes, transition – that's it.

Counsellor: Okay, let's see if we have this straight now. You need to **be** with your family more *(the word 'be' is heavily emphasised)* and yet work places many demands on your time – but even so, a little more time to make the transition from work mode to family mode would be good. So then you can attend to family stuff more. Does that sound right?

Client: *(long pause)* Yes. I think so, yes.

Counsellor: Okay, well, you've already told me that if you don't do this, you might end up losing your family so is that the main reason? What is spending more time with your family going to do for you?

Client: I'm not sure really. *(pause)* Well, yes, I suppose that's the main reason. I don't want to lose Dave – that would be really

151

	sad but I know I've got to make more effort.
Counsellor:	Okay, well, fear's a pretty strong motivator but what else will spending more time attending to your family more fully, what else will that do for you?
Client:	Well, I suppose I should say it would make me happier but then I think about it and I'm not sure it would. It sounds awful but sometimes I think I really don't care. I'm not really interested in family life. God, isn't that terrible! Maybe Dave should leave me.
Counsellor:	You know, people usually find that the most important things in life are those things they spend most time involved with. Sometimes we need to step outside to see what really matters.
Client:	You mean like, because I spend so much time with work, then that's what's important to me? If I spent more time with family, then that would become more important?
Counsellor:	Something like that, yes.
Client:	Well, I suppose that sounds logical although it's hard to imagine right now.
Counsellor:	Okay, well, let's perhaps assume that it will work like that. Now, what would that do for you?
Client:	More balance ... more ... I guess it could be more fun.
Counsellor:	You mean you don't have fun at work?
Client:	God no! Work is hell most of the time *(smile)*.
Counsellor:	*(smiling)* That must be why you want to spend so much time there then.
Client:	*(grinning)* God – that makes me sound like a right miserable cow, doesn't it. Yes, maybe spending more time with family, I can start to laugh a bit more, get things into perspective a little.
Counsellor:	Well, perspective's important *(long pause)*. So gaining some perspective, getting some fun back into your life. What would that do for you?
Client:	*(long pause)* Hmmph! Isn't it amazing how life becomes so twisted like you start out with ideas about what you want and stuff and suddenly it's all gone, like it's just evaporated away.

Counsellor: Yes, that does happen.

Client: Okay, I'm not answering your question am I?

Counsellor: That's okay – just stay with it.

Client: Well, when I ask myself that question it seems pretty obvious and I think I must be really stupid not to have realised before.

Counsellor: I think that's a little harsh. There's been lots to distract you.

Client: Tell me about it! *(smile)* That's what it's all about really, isn't it. I mean, I need to spend more time with my family because otherwise what's the point in anything. Family and friends – they're really the things that matter. Or at least they should matter. I need to remember why that matters.

Counsellor: Okay, let's suppose you achieve this. Let's suppose for a moment that you find ways to spend more time with your family, time to make the transition to family mode so that you're more attentive – and in doing that you start to appreciate how important family is again and maybe get some perspective back on life. If all of this were to happen, how would you know when you'd achieved it? How would things be different?

Client: Well, obviously there's the time factor. I mean, that can be measured, like if I was leaving work earlier. Dave wouldn't be threatening to leave me, we'd be happier together. I don't know, I suppose that's about it, really.

Counsellor: Do you think you would feel any different?

Client: Well, yes. I'd be happier, less hassled. I'd feel more secure I suppose, less panicky.

Counsellor: And, if I were to meet you again somewhere in the future when you'd achieved all of this, how would I know? What would I see that would be different?

Client: I'm not sure. Maybe you'd see me laughing more, looking more relaxed. I don't know. Maybe even more interesting to be with, you know – not moaning all the time. *(smile)*

Counsellor: Now, when did I ever say you moaned all the while? *(smile)* Okay, now let me just check something with you. Changing how you make use of your time so you spend more time with your family. That means you're going to be attending to them

	more, thinking about them more and so on. What about when you're at work – what if you spend so much time thinking about family things, you don't get any work done?
Client:	Well, obviously I don't want to go too far. It's about balance isn't it? When I'm at work, I still need to be able to concentrate on work. It's just that when I'm at home, I need to be properly at home.
Counsellor:	That's okay. I was just being especially careful. Sometimes people make changes and forget about the context or how appropriate those changes are throughout the rest of their lives and then they can come unstuck.
Client:	Yes, I see what you mean but, no, I realise that I can't change all of this over night.
Counsellor:	Okay, well then, what is stopping you making this change right now?
Client:	It's going to take a little planning and I have to get the guys at work used to the idea that I'm not going to be around so much.
Counsellor:	Is that a problem? You know, at work – are there going to be people who make it hard for you?
Client:	Well, it's possible I suppose, although everyone always says I work far too many hours.
Counsellor:	Mmm … sounds like the sort of thing that's easy to say but how will they be when they don't get what they need when they expect it?
Client:	Well, they might put some pressure on me but ultimately they won't be able to stop me. I'll need to talk to some of them, explain how things are going to be. The biggest problem will be towards the end of each month. That's always very busy.
Counsellor:	Okay, so there are things you need to do at work. Is there anything else that might get in the way of your achieving this?
Client:	No, no, I don't think so. Except maybe me, I suppose.
Counsellor:	How do you mean?
Client:	Well, you know, it's easy making all these resolutions sitting here but once I'm back in work mode, I'll probably forget all this.

Counsellor:	That's really about motivation isn't it? We can do stuff to help you with that, you know, so you don't forget how important this change is even when you're snowed under at work.
Client:	Yes please, that would be really important. *(smiles)* I know me.
Counsellor:	Well, I guess we've pretty much covered that but, just one final question. Is there anything else? Is there anything at all that might result from this change that wouldn't be welcome by either you or anyone else?
Client:	I'm not sure I understand what you're asking.
Counsellor:	Well, could there be any negative consequences of taking this action, maybe things you might not have considered yet? We've mentioned work and got that pretty much covered, I think.
Client:	*(long pause)* No, I don't think so. I can't think of anything. *(pause)* Can you?
Counsellor:	*(smiles)* How would I know? *(laughs)* Okay, I suppose what I was thinking was how is this going to impact on your family and friends because from here it all sounds very positive but even positive change can have some negative impact.
Client:	Well, I guess they could get sick and tired of me hanging around the house all the time. *(laughs)*
Counsellor:	Well, it does happen you know *(smiles)* even though I'm sure they love you very much and love having you home, it does alter the balance a little.
Client:	Well, yes, I suppose it does. I'd not really thought about it like that.
Counsellor:	Okay, don't let it stop you making this change, but perhaps be a little sensitive to things like this just in case.
Client:	Yes, yes I will.

10

Therapeutic Counselling

Therapeutic counselling is much more concerned with bringing about change within the client's own behaviour, thinking and feeling. I include under this umbrella label all types of more involved counselling and psychotherapy in as much as they are intended to bring about these changes through the use of one-to-one or group interaction. At one end of the spectrum we have the Freudian and Neo-Freudian approaches of psychoanalysis where the emphasis is very much on the relationship between therapist and client and the client's ability to learn to manage his or her own internal processes when relating to the therapist. And, at the other end we have psychotherapeutic approaches such as behavioural and cognitive therapy that aim very much more at making specific changes to behaviour and thinking through the application of specific techniques.

In its fullest form, **systemic counselling** is psychotherapeutic. It helps bring about changes in clients' behaviour, thinking and feeling by working directly with the clients' models of the world and more importantly, their modelling of the world.

In this chapter, I want to introduce the **psychotherapeutic aspects** of systemic counselling by way of example. Rather than simply give an overview of what is involved, I believe it more useful to provide you the reader with a slightly more in-depth insight into the more complex world of therapeutic counselling. To do this I have selected a session transcript taken from session one of a series of sessions with a production manager of a large factory. Firstly this is not intended to cover all aspects of therapeutic counselling; in realty it actually covers a tiny fraction of all that is included within therapeutic counselling.

Secondly, it is not presented as a 'perfect' piece of work. Throughout the session, the counsellor makes choices that are not necessarily the 'best' choices but are nevertheless very much the sort of choices systemic counsellors typically take. Lastly, the session is not complete – this is not by any means all that is needed to help this man resolve the issues he is having within his life.

I will also introduce the Lifegrid, one of the major modelling tools utilised by systemic counsellors, and we shall use this as a means of tracking and understanding what takes place within the example session.

The Lifegrid

The Lifegrid is one of the key DBM modelling tools used by systemic counsellors. As a modelling tool, it has a wide variety of uses and applications, but there is no single 'right' way to use the Lifegrid. Experienced systemic counsellors will often use the Lifegrid as a key conceptual tool in organising their subjective understanding of a client's world. They needn't necessarily make explicit use of it as for them it becomes very much a natural tool for understanding their clients. By contrast, the novice systemic counsellor is encouraged to make more explicit use of the Lifegrid by literally using the grid as a way of mapping out the various aspects and dynamics of the client's problem. When used in training exercises, participants are often given laminated Lifegrids to practice with making it easy to wipe out mistakes or dead end pieces of modelling.

For the purposes of this chapter, we shall be using the Lifegrid to help shed light on the piece of change work that takes place within the transcripted client session.

The Lifegrid is a grid made up of an x and y axis with a series of distinctions along each, cross referencing to draw out the grid. See fig 15. The y axis marks out various levels of processing which will be explained in more detail shortly. The y axis is complete and all-inclusive; as such it is rarely changed. The distinctions on the x axis on the other hand are less fixed and, although we shall use a fairly standard configuration, it can and often is modified. The distinctions on the x access are concerned with the various systems or areas of the client's life and include self, family, work and social. These distinctions are fairly self explanatory.

Level \ Area	Self	Other	Home	Work	Social	System
Overman						
Identity						
Belief						
Values toward / away						
Capabilities						
Experience						
Behaviour — Concepts						
Behaviour — Language						
Behaviour — Senses						
Behaviour — Movement						
Environment						

Figure 15

So, if we look more closely at the y axis, we see, as has already been stated, that it consists of a series of divisions that correspond to levels of processing, beginning at the bottom with **environment** and working all the way up to a level labelled **overman**. These are best explained and understood in terms of a developmental sequence. That is to say that they correspond with the sequence in which processing develops from birth, through childhood and on into adulthood.

A newly born child responds primarily to its own physical state; it may be hungry, it may be wet or it could be experiencing some other kind of physiological sensation. This physiological state is the child's individual **environment,** the first level of processing found at the bottom of the grid and it is the first type of processing to develop. For the individual then, environment is the physical self and of course the state of this physical self has a big impact of the individual's functioning. If we work across the areas of the grid then obviously what constitutes 'environment' changes. For the family, environment equates with the home they live in, for work it is the physical workplace.

The following four levels come under the more general heading of **behaviour**.

As the child grows it begins to develop greater control over its **movement** and as it does so, it learns to move in response to changes in its environment. If it is environmentally uncomfortable in one position, it can move in order to become more comfortable. Movement organises its environment and it is a general feature of the levels of the Lifegrid that higher levels, although developing from lower levels, then organise those lower levels.

As the child develops further it learns to **sense** the world using its five senses. The child learns to use its senses to gather information from the world so that it can respond and move in response. Thus, movement follows sensing or, sensing organises movement. The child hears a sound and moves in response, it moves its head, its eyes leading the way. The child can then represent the world it experiences subjectively through further use of the senses (See Chapter 3)

From the vast mass of sensory data, the child learns to abstract and simplify with the acquisition of **language**. Objects have names and relate to one another in numerous dynamic ways. Through language, the child can begin to construct meaning from the world of sensory experience. Our use of language then begins to organise how we sense the world. Language becomes prescriptive of sensory experience. The experience of encountering a dog becomes changed once we have the label 'dog' to use. Language becomes added to our thinking and we can enrich our internal representation of the world though its use.

As we grow and our use of language becomes more sophisticated, we begin to categorise the experiences we have until we are eventually able to represent these categories through the even more abstract use of **concepts**. For example, after we have experienced seeing many birds, we eventually form a concept of 'bird' which becomes a useful shorthand in our thinking, capturing the very essence of birdness. Conceptual thinking is the most sophisticated human behaviour and develops to a greater or lesser extent in all humans.

Language and concepts provide us with meaning and once we have this ability we can then have meaningful **experience** we can draw upon in our progress through life. Our ongoing experience will now help organise the ways in which we behave. For example, a child growing up in an East Coast fishing village will develop different concepts and language use to the child growing up in the heart of a large city.

Certain repeatable experiences become **skills, capabilities** or **habits** and these are unique to each child. When used in this context, no value judgement is placed on these capabilities. The systemic counsellor is equally concerned with skills, capabilities and habits that limit as he is with those that enhance. People can become very skilled at their problems. The skills, capabilities and habits we develop over time play a large part in determining our future experience.

As the child develops further, it begins to find pleasure and reward in some experience and displeasure in others. Some things the child learns to **value**. Another way of thinking about values is in terms of basic orientations either away from or towards the experiences a child has. These become powerful motivators as the child is drawn towards the more positive orientations or values and away from the negative. As the child becomes more mature, it develops the ability to more actively seek out experiences it values and avoid or move away from those it doesn't. If the child has a strong moving towards value for something, it will want to spend more time with it. It will learn the skills and languages associated with the experience. The child's senses will become attuned to noticing what it values and it will find itself physically moving towards these.

The child begins to develop certain **beliefs** and belief systems about itself and its world. These are often beliefs about what is possibly, probably or necessarily the case within the child's understanding of the world. How and what the growing child believes in this way will have a dramatic impact upon its functioning within the world, affecting all of the lower levels of processing.

Some beliefs become more fixed and certain. Some things the child begins to know with absolute conviction; its sense of self and who it is being a good example. The child does not believe its sense of self, it does not believe it is who it is, it knows who it is. It has a sense of **identity**. Equally it identifies other things in its world which help give it a sense of solidity and certainty. As I sit writing this, I know that the sun is in the sky, that if I head cast I will eventually reach the sea, that the chair I am sitting on supports me. These are not issues of belief but rather of **Identity**. It is how the world is.

Finally, we have to account for the fact that, for many growing up in our world, there are issues that become more important than our individual identity. These are issues not just about being but about becoming something more. This often manifests itself in a person developing a higher sense of purpose in life. For many this becomes spiritual or religious but it doesn't have to be. We call this level **overman** or **om**, a term first used and described by the German philosopher Nietzsche.

For any given problem, all of these levels of processing will be involved, some more so than others. The dynamic interplay between the levels is also important. Effective therapeutic work aims to make changes in processing at the appropriate levels but the systemic counsellor should not fall into the trap of oversimplifying and believing that only one level is important in any given situation.

We shall use the Lifegrid to model what takes place in the following transcript. I suggest you read fully through the transcript first to get a general feel for what is taking place before going on to look at the Lifegrid analysis. In looking at the analysis, consider how it helps highlight what is significant in the client's story.

Therapeutic counselling transcript

The following transcript is based on actual systemic counselling sessions although the client is not named to help preserve anonymity. This is session one of a six session series. Some parts have been omitted in order to focus on the important elements of the change work. The reader will notice many similarities between this client's presenting issues and the client's problem from the last chapter. This has been deliberate and helps to highlight the fact that similarities in content are often superficial. A very different approach is employed with this client.

Counsellor: Good morning. How are you?

Client: I'm very well thank you and you?

Counsellor: Yes, I'm good thanks. *(At this point, the counsellor goes through some administrative details and sets out for the client what he can expect from counselling. We take up the session again once these preliminaries are out of the way)* Now, I have this referral report here from the Occupational Health Department. Perhaps if I tell you what they have to say about you and then we can take it form there – okay?

Client: Yes, that sounds fine.

Counsellor: Okay, well, let's have a look. It says here that you're a senior manager in production and that you have an excellent work record and no history of any major health problems. You visited the Occupational Health Department one month ago complaining of persistent and repeating headaches. During their assessment, it transpired that you had been experiencing other symptoms such as sleeplessness for several weeks and that two days earlier while preparing for a meeting, you had experienced what sounds like a panic attack. Was that the first time you've had one of those?

Client: Well, yes, yes it was, really. I suppose when I was younger, when I was at university, I had a spell that felt similar – you know, getting anxious for no apparent reason and things like that, but that was a long time ago and feels like that was different somehow.

Counsellor: But you recognised it as a panic attack?

Client: Oh yes, my mother used to suffer from them so I realised what was happening straight away.

Counsellor: Okay, now, it says that you are happy in your work and couldn't think of anything that might have triggered this, or indeed anything that might account for the headaches and the sleeplessness.

Client: Yes, that's right.

Counsellor: And you spent some time with the Occupational Health Doctor and you both agreed that part of your problem was that you worked too much, you spent too much time at work and not enough with your family. So, you planned to spend some more time with your family, try to get home earlier in the evenings, that sort of thing.

Client: Yes, it seemed pretty straight forward at the time, made a lot of sense. I know I have been spending too much time at work and not enough with Cath and the kids.

Counsellor: So, when you say too long, what would an average day be like, you know what sort of time would you get home?

Client: Well, I like to get an early start so I'm usually in the office by about 7.30 and then I guess ... well, perhaps I'd better explain – you see, we have a big upgrade project going on at the moment so this isn't really normal but I suppose I get home for about eight thirty, nineish.

Counsellor: Yes, I see, that is a long day – you must love your work.

Client: Well, yes I do, *(smiling)* but it's not just that. If we don't get this right, the company could really suffer so I have to do my bit you know.

Counsellor: Okay, well, that's about all I know about you so perhaps you can fill me in with the rest. What brings you here? What are you wanting from me?

Client: Mmm ... okay, well, let's see. Well, after I went to Occupational Health I tried to put what we'd discussed into practice but it doesn't seem to have made much difference – I suppose that's why they decided to send me to you.

Counsellor: And how do you feel about that?

Client: About seeing you? Yes, I'm fine with that. I'm not sure it will help but I'll give it a shot.

Counsellor: Well, the implication of seeing me is that this is some kind of stress-related problem; certainly the panic attack would suggest that.

Client: Well, maybe, but I must say I can't think of anything stressful going on at the moment. I don't find work particularly stressful, it's a challenge alright but that's how I like it. I suppose that's one of the reasons this has taken me by surprise, I mean it's not just the panic attack and the insomnia. I have to say I have been feeling quite low at times. I'd say it feels more like I might be depressed than stressed. but you're the expert.

Counsellor: I don't think it matters too much what we call it. These terms aren't precise. Depression, stress, whatever – the important thing is that you don't feel quite yourself and we need to look at how we can help you get over that and get things back on track. So, tell me about what you've tried already. The plan you agreed with the Occupational Health doctor.

Client: Yes, okay then – well, he suggested I should spend more time with Cath and the kids, more quality time. I suppose I feel quite bad really that I'd not been spending time with them. You know, we haven't really done things together as a family for, god, I don't know, ages I suppose. I think he thought that I needed something other than just work to focus on, something that would take my mind off work. I suppose in one way that makes sense but, like I said, it's not like I'm finding work particularly stressful. Anyway, he's right, family is important and I should spend more time with them. So I went away from there and spent some time going over my schedule to try and free up some time, some regular time. That wasn't easy, what with Cath's evening classes and then the kids have Karate and Scouts and stuff, but I found a slot on Thursday evenings where we could do things together as a family.

Counsellor: You found a slot?

Client: Yes, well like I said, it wasn't easy to find some time when everyone was free but I managed to re-arrange some regular

meetings and free up a couple of hours on Thursday
afternoons which meant I could go home early and we could
do something together as a family.

Counsellor: *(Smiling)* You managed to free up a couple of hours, and did
you have your secretary come along and take minutes.

Client: *(Sniggers)* I know it sounds awful doesn't it, like they're
another business meeting or something but really, it was the
only way.

Counsellor: Sure, I know, I was only kidding along but it does make you
wonder doesn't it about what's important and where we place
our priorities and so on.

Client: Mmm … *(long pause)* actually it makes me feel really quite
sad. *(further pause)* Anyway, we've been doing stuff, you
know like the cinema or going to Pizza Hut and things like
that for a few weeks now, and I suppose the kids like it and it
does make a change, but I'm not really feeling any different.
(further pause) I'm sorry, I'm not sure what's come over me.
I'm actually feeling quite upset. *(longer pause)* I suppose
that's it really, I feel kind of lost, you know not quite sure what
it's all about any more. No, that sounds rather too
melodramatic, not lost but, you know, questioning and not
really knowing I'm doing it but waking up in the mornings and
feeling really low and wondering why I bother. And, I can't
understand it because I've always really loved my work.

Counsellor: It often happens when we start to experience thoughts and
emotions that make us uncomfortable. We kind of pretend
they're not really happening.

Client: Well I could understand it if I was hard up or out of work or
something but I'm a really lucky guy. I've got a great job, a
lovely wife and kids, things are really fine so what have I got
to feel depressed about?

Counsellor: So, what, you think only poor people feel depressed?

Client: No, no of course not. I know it's not that simple but really, I
haven't got anything to feel depressed about – I mean I have
everything a man could want.

Counsellor: Okay, it might seem that way but clearly something's not

	quite right. Tell me, after you've spent your Thursday evenings with the family, how do you then feel, afterwards and the next morning?
Client:	Not sure really. No different I think. It's difficult. I mean, last week we went to the cinema but I couldn't really switch off. There was a report I'd had to leave half finished and I kept thinking about how I was going to finish it.
Counsellor:	What was the film?
Client:	The film?
Counsellor:	Yes, the film. The film you saw at the cinema.
Client:	Oh yeah that, it was a family comedy ... *(pause)* trying to remember what it was called.
Counsellor:	It doesn't really matter, I was just curious. Did you all enjoy it?
Client:	No, not really. It wasn't my sort of thing; I found it hard to concentrate. But, I think the kids enjoyed it.
Counsellor:	You think they enjoyed it. Did they say whether they did?
Client:	You know I'm not sure. They must have done I suppose but after we got home, I was so tired I had to go to bed early and then I haven't really spoken to them since then.
Counsellor:	Okay, well,l this is maybe going to sound like a silly question but, do you enjoy spending time with your family?
Client:	Of course I do, I love them very much.
Counsellor:	Oh, don't get me wrong, I'm quite sure you do love them very much but that's not the same thing as enjoying being with them.
Client:	No, no I realise that but, of course I mean that's what it's all about at the end of the day isn't it? It's what we work for, for the family and being with them. You know, you achieve all this so that you can give them the things they need and help them enjoy life and enjoy things together, That's how it should be.
Counsellor:	Okay, I think I understand that. It's how it should be right?
Client:	Yes, I can't think that there's anything more important. I mean, I'm not a religious man or anything like that.
Counsellor:	Okay, well, that's how it should be but, and this is a really important question I'm going to ask now. *(pause)* Is that how

it is? Do you actually enjoy spending time with your family? And, think about that for a bit before you answer.

Client: Mmm that's a really tough question. If I'm really, really honest, then I guess it has to be no. That's awful – I can't believe I'm saying that. What kind of a father am I?

Counsellor: Well, don't be too hard on yourself here, there are very many reasons why you might feel that way just at the moment.

Client: I thought about leaving you know. Getting a divorce. Not seriously, I don't think, but as an option. I mean, if I'm not happy and not spending time with them, then what's the point in hanging around?

Counsellor: And, would that solve anything?

Client: No, not really, it was just a passing thought.

Counsellor: And, what does your wife, what does Cath make of all this?

Client: I'm not sure ... I mean, I don't really talk to her about it she has enough on her plate with the kids and everything. I think she knows something isn't right – she's asked me a few times if everything is alright at work, that sort of thing and she's been fussing about me more than usual but it's hard to talk to her about this sort of thing. I mean. what do I say? I'm unhappy, I want to leave! I'm sure she's going to respond well to that.

Counsellor: I'm sorry, I'm getting a little confused here. I thought you said you didn't really want to leave.

Client: No, no, I don't not really but I suppose, well, I might end up saying something I'd regret if I started to talk to her about these things. She's not the best listener in the world and she'd probably get the wrong end of the stick or something.

Counsellor: Okay, at some level you're unhappy, possibly depressed or stressed or something like that but you're not really sure why or what that's about. You work hard and spend long hours at the office which you enjoy and find challenging. You feel you should spend more time with the family but when you do spend time with them, you're still thinking more about work and in any case you don't really enjoy doing things with the family even though you think you should. Actually from what

you said, it sounds like that's something you really think is important, it's what it's all about. And, so even though you enjoy your work, life feels a little empty?

Client: Mmm empty ... not sure ... not sure if that's quite the feeling.

Counsellor: Well, no, that was my word, me trying to find someway to describe how you feel.

Client: No, no, I mean yes – that's actually quite a good way of describing it, empty. When I really think about it I suppose that is pretty much how I feel. Kind of empty and pointless. I mean, I take pride in my work but then I think so what? What if I wasn't there any more – would I really be missed? It's kind of a lonely feeling.

Counsellor: And you want to feel fulfilled, important, like you matter – is that it?

Client: Kind of, like what I'm doing is for a reason, a reason that matters. I think, I'm not sure – I mean, I have all that don't I, a family and a nice lifestyle and a good job.

Counsellor: In a sense you do but in another way you don't really do you?

Client: Not sure what you mean.

Counsellor: Well, objectively you have all of that. Anyone could come along and take a look and verify that you have a good lifestyle and all of that but that's not really your experience of it. Like when you went to the cinema, objectively you were with your family but on another level you weren't, at least your attention was not on them, with them, it was still on your work. So in that sense you're not really getting anything from all of this good lifestyle stuff at all, it's just not part of where your head is at.

Client: Yes, yes, that makes a lot of sense. *(lengthy pause)* I'm not sure I like it though, I mean I'm not sure I like myself very much when I think that's how I am. How can a man not be interested in or take pleasure form being with his family? That makes me sound awful.

Counsellor: Okay, and that's another issue really but maybe it explains some of why you've been feeling low. But can you perhaps see that at some deeper level, you don't really value your work for its own sake that highly, even though you find it enjoyable and challenging, and so you look for something more valuable, more important and think that really should be your wife and kids and family life but your experience doesn't really back that up.

Client: Mmm yes I can kind of follow that. It's not easy, though.

Counsellor: Well, let's see if we can clarify things further. Let's simplify it a little and see where that gets us.

Client: Ok

Counsellor: What I'm thinking is that it's as if you spend all your time working in order to fulfil some dream – like if you were doing it so that you could afford to buy really expensive hi-fi equipment and a huge collection of CDs, something like that. And yet, when you really think about it, you don't really enjoy listening to the music much in any case, you find it hard to just relax and enjoy and usually end up thinking more about your work. Anyway, you have to find some way to motivate yourself to work, so as well as telling yourself that you can buy some new CD or some new piece of hi-fi, which you think should be motivation enough but really isn't, you look for satisfaction in the work itself. Over time, you make your work matter, it becomes more important than anything else, it's where you get your kicks, your buzz, it's where all the really interesting things happen in life and when you're back home listening to another boring CD, it's no wonder that your attention drifts back to work. Except deep down you know your job isn't so important, not so important that it should occupy your whole life.

Client: *(Long pause)* Mmmm … I can see that, I mean it makes so much sense. *(Long pause)* I suppose I've become kind of mixed up about what matters. *(Shakes head slowly)* It's amazing isn't it – I mean, it all seems so straightforward and easy on the surface. Get a good job, find a wife, raise a family that sort of thing.

This is a good point at which to take a break from the transcript and begin piecing things together using the Lifegrid. Both the client and the counsellor seem to have arrived at an understanding of the problem. Here is a Lifegrid representation of that understanding together with a key to further explain the letters used.

Level \ Area	Self	Other	Home	Work	Social	System
Overman						
Identity	①					
Belief	Ⓖ Ⓗ					
Values toward / away	Ⓕ Ⓔ					
Capabilities						
Experience	Ⓓ Ⓒ	Ⓐ		Ⓑ		
Behaviour — Concepts						
Behaviour — Language						
Behaviour — Senses						
Behaviour — Movement						
Environment						

Figure 16

A   The family experience (going to the cinema).

B   The work experience.

C   The client's experience of being with the family. This is a negative experience reinforcing the moving away from value E below. When pressed with the question, 'Do you actually enjoy spending time with your family?' he answers, 'If I'm really honest, then I guess it has to be no.'

170

D   The client's experience of being at work. This is a positive experience reinforcing the moving towards value F below. He describes work as '... a challenge all right, but that's how I like it.'

E   *Away* value of being with family. The client does not enjoy (value) being with his family.

F   *Towards* value of being with work. The client enjoys (values) being at work. When talking about a night out with his family, the client explains that 'there was a report I had to leave half finished and I kept thinking about how I was going to finish it.'

G   The belief that spending time with family is important. The client states clearly and on several occasions that it is important that he spends time with his family. He says at one point, 'I know I have been spending too much time at work and not enough with Cath and the kids.' and later '... family is important and I should spend more time with them.' On first reading, these may seem more like values than beliefs but note how they are much more statements about how things should be than actual descriptions of his experience. If he described his experience with his family as something he enjoyed and wanted to spend more time doing, then it would be more likely that this would be something he valued.

H   The client believes that ultimately what he does at work is of no real significance. When reflecting on work he says, 'I take pride in my work but then I think so what? I mean what if I wasn't there any more would I really be missed?'

I   This double conflict between what he believes is important and what he actually finds himself enjoying and engaging in leads to feelings of emptiness, loneliness and pointlessness. These bring about important questions about who he actually is and the purpose of his life. These are identity issues. It also brings into question his role as a family member and father and at one point he asks the rhetorical question, 'How can a man not be interested in or take pleasure form being with his family? That makes me sound awful.'

171

Interestingly, the client has considered the rather drastic and potentially disastrous solution of leaving his wife and family. This is an excellent example of the kind of problem being a solution we explored in the previous chapter where action is taken when it should not be.

As we continue with the transcript note how the counsellor utilises this growing understanding to begin the process of change.

Counsellor:	I'm not so sure. If it were really that easy, why are there so many unhappy people around – and there are, I meet most of them.
Client:	(Smiling) I'm sure you do. This is actually really useful. The more I think about it, I suppose I'm just not sure what to do about it. I mean, it's one thing understanding but what to do?
Counsellor:	Well, it's an understanding; let's not get too carried away believing that's all there is to it or that this is the only way to think about this.
Client:	No, no, I realise that but, it's better than just being confused all the time or not knowing. I'm just not sure where to go from here.
Counsellor:	Again, maybe there isn't just one way to go. Maybe there are many options and maybe there are lots of different things that have to be done.
Client:	Okay well, I can understand that, I think, but we have to start somewhere don't we so what do you suggest?
Counsellor:	Well, one of the things I know to be the case is that we learn to value things and our values can and do change, usually completely outside of our awareness. So, there was probably a time, maybe a good while ago now, when the very thought of spending the day writing reports and attending meetings would have seemed really boring and unattractive and yet somewhere along the line you learned to value these activities.
Client:	You mean like when I was a teenager or something, that far back?
Counsellor:	Yes, I mean tastes change. When you were a kid, there were

	probably foods you didn't like, maybe vegetables or something like that and yet later, when you were much older you tried them again and found that you liked them.
Client:	Lettuce, *(smiles)* well, any salad really.
Counsellor:	Yup, that's a favourite. So anyway, it sounds to me like it might be useful as a starting point to learn to really value time with your family and not just the idea. So that the actual experience of being with them is its own reward, becoming increasingly important.
Client:	Sounds good, how do we do that?
Counsellor:	Well, whatever we do, it's not going to happen overnight – you must understand that.
Client:	Oh yes, I realise that.
Counsellor:	Okay, let's suppose then we start with a little more exploration – let's look a little more closely at some of these beliefs and values and things you have.
Client:	Okay.
Counsellor:	Well, you mentioned that being with your family is important or at least should be important and I'm not quite sure how you came to believe that, but what is so important about being with your family?
Client:	Mmm ... I'm going to need to think about that.
Counsellor:	It's okay – take your time, there really is no rush and if we don't have time to finish this today we'll just carry on next time. You really do need to take your time over this and consider it fully... really wonder and ponder over your answers.
Client:	Well, I want to say that that's just the way it should be, I'm finding it hard to think beyond that really.
Counsellor:	Okay, stay with it. What's important that it should be that way?
Client:	Well, I suppose in a way it's a mark of your success isn't it? If you can have a successful marriage and raise your children to be happy and enjoy life, be successful, then you should be able to take some satisfaction from that.
Counsellor:	Like a job well done?

Client:	Yes, something like that, I suppose.
Counsellor:	Like a successful business meeting?
Client:	Well, yes, but not quite so ... oh, I don't know – I'm thinking not as important, but that's nonsense of course. It's more important but it's like somehow you can be more relaxed over family stuff – like making a mistake or cocking up isn't the end of the world.
Counsellor:	You're under less pressure, maybe?
Client:	Yes, yes, I think so, yes, less pressure but otherwise it is very similar, I suppose.
Counsellor:	Okay, but it strikes me that you can't ever know you've made a success of it all until, oh, I don't know, until your lives are over really. How can you know that you're succeeding actually at the time you're with them, doing stuff together?
Client:	Yes, I'm with you, well I suppose you don't really do you, I mean, as long as everyone is happy, achieving stuff at school, behaving themselves and that kind of thing then, well then you know you must be doing something right.
Counsellor:	And of course to do that you do have to spend time with them and pay attention when you're with them.
Client:	Yes, but now it's sounding a little too much like work, you know it's like I'm setting performance target for them *(Smiles)*
Counsellor:	Well, you do enjoy your work so I suppose one way of enjoying time with your family would be making it more like work.
Client:	Heaven forbid, Cath would never forgive me – *(laughs)* no really that would be bad. I wouldn't want to inflict that on them.
Counsellor:	Yes, and you've already said raising a family is more relaxed than work so I suppose you wouldn't want to spoil that. So, spending time and attending and being relaxed, what's important about all of those?
Client:	Well then, you should be able to enjoy it shouldn't you, if you have all of those then being with them should be enjoyable.
Counsellor:	Okay, so what's important about enjoying spending time with them?

Client: Oh goodness, well if you don't then what's the point?

Counsellor: And you don't. *(Long pause)*

Client: Mmmm ... now I feel like I'm going round in circles, like I should enjoy it but I don't.

Counsellor: Stay with it. Let's look at it another way. What is enjoyable, currently, I mean right now, what is enjoyable about being with them? Anything even if it doesn't seems like very much.

Client: That's tough, I'm trying to think.

Counsellor: Maybe think back to last week, going to the cinema. I know you've already said that you didn't really enjoy it but it can't all have been bad – there must have been some bits that were more enjoyable than others.

Client: Well, yes, it's always good to see the children happy. I'm not sure it's enjoyment as such but it warms the heart *(grins)*.

Counsellor: And they were happy?

Client: Well, yes, I think so.

Counsellor: I wonder, can you imagine how it would be if they were the opposite, you know if they were really unhappy and not enjoying anything.

Client: Mmm ... yes that makes me really sad, I'd rather not dwell on that.

Counsellor: Well, It's fortunate then that they were happy when you were with them because even though it doesn't seem like very much at first you only have to consider the opposite to realise how important it is to you that they are happy. Now, is that feeling, that feeling you get when they are obviously happy, that warm feeling, is that anything like enjoyment?

Client: Well, it is, yes, I suppose, something like enjoyment. It's very easy to take these things for granted. But, it's nothing like the buzz I get from work.

Counsellor: Okay, but it's a start, yes?

Client: Yes, it's a start.

Counsellor: Something we'll build on. So, let's think about the buzz a little more. Tell me, what does that feel like?

Client: Well, like I'm really alive, you know, energised and ready to take on anything. It's excitement like what I'm doing matters.

Counsellor:	And, have you ever felt this way in your home life, at anytime in the past? Even a little bit or something similar.
Client:	Yes, sometimes, if I'm working on a project like fitting the new kitchen or something like that.
Counsellor:	That's interesting because I suppose that's a lot like the kind of thing you do at work. I don't mean fitting kitchens as such but you know it has a clear goal, an end result which is either successful or not. Like you said, it's a project.
Client:	Yes, I like anything like that really. As long as I know where I'm going and can just get on with it.
Counsellor:	And, being with your family, enjoying time doing things with them – that's not like a project, there's no clear end result.
Client:	Well, I suppose you could look at raising the kids as being a bit like a project but it's not really the same.
Counsellor:	No, of course not, it's infinitely more varied and open ended. Much more challenging in that respect.
Client:	Yes I've never really thought about it like that before, but yes, I suppose it is.
Counsellor:	Okay, well, stay with that feeling for a moment. What would you call that feeling?
Client:	Sorry, I'm not sure I'm with you, what feeling do you mean?
Counsellor:	Just then, when I mentioned how varied and open ended the challenge of raising kids was you seem to become quite … animated, your face kind of became more intense, like you were experiencing quite a strong feeling.
Client:	Yes, yes, I suppose I was, well just for a minute, I think it was when you said challenging – it was like I suddenly felt very strong and determined, you know, like someone has thrown down the gauntlet.
Counsellor:	Okay, so stay with that feeling, just keep it there in the background.
Client:	Uh huh, yes, that's easy enough.
Counsellor:	Now, I want you to think about last week and going to the cinema with Cath and the kids, but not so much as it was, but more feeling the way you do now. With that feeling in the background, how would that have been different? Kind of

reliving the experience but with this different feeling.

Client: *(Long pause)* Yes that's actually very different ... paying more attention ... feels much better ... more connected somehow.

Counsellor: Okay, and what happens to that feeling as you pay more attention in that way?

Client: Yes, it's good ... much better, really.

Counsellor: That's how you feel about the feeling and that's good, but tell me about the actual feeling itself – does that change in anyway?

Client: Mmm ... it becomes stronger, more ... no not really stronger ... mmm, that's really quite strange because it's almost like it goes away, but I feel this real warmth, you know, being with the kids and it's a really happy feeling ... I don't know. I really don't have words.

Counsellor: Good, that's good and does it take any effort at all to maintain that feeling?

Client: No, no, I don't think so – it's just there.

Counsellor: So okay, now, leave that memory in the past and let's think about this coming Thursday. Do you have anything planned for this Thursday?

Client: Yes, I think we're supposed to be going out for a pizza, something like that.

Counsellor: Right, well, first go back to that initial feeling, the one you had when the gauntlet was thrown down.

Client: Yes, yes, that's easy.

Counsellor: Now again, keep that feeling very much there in the background and imagine stepping into the future on Thursday night and even though you don't know precisely all the details, how is it when you imagine how that will be?

Client: *(Pause)* Yes, very similar, very, very similar. That's really very good – I'm actually quite looking forward to it *(Smiles)*.

Counsellor: Okay, let's just see where we're at with all of this. It seems to me that learning to value being with your family would be a very worthwhile project to embark on. I think we'll both know when you've started achieving more success in this, and you've made a start. Enjoyment is not black and white, you know, it's not about whether you enjoy something or not but more about how much you enjoy or what aspects were more enjoyable than others, and once you start to see it more that way, it becomes easy to find enjoyments in being with your family and, who knows, maybe even get a buzz from it, albeit a slightly different kind of buzz. It won't replace work, it shouldn't, but it will complement work. You'll still get that special buzz from work but it won't be the only pleasure. Maybe you'll have to become a little more creative as you do that. Rather than waiting for the meaning or the importance to find you, you going out and creating it.

Client: Mmm ... yes, thank you. Lots to think about.

At first it seems as though the counsellor is heading in a dead end direction as he questions the client more about the structure behind the belief that it is important to spend time with the family. The client struggles to think beyond the idea that it is important because that's just how it should be and feels he is going in circles. However, what the counsellor has succeeded in doing is raising the client's awareness of just how important learning to enjoy being with his family really is and this provides a powerful motivator for the following piece of change work.

This Lifegrid model below (figure 17) also includes numbered arrows to help sequence the dynamics of the change work. The reader will see how the piece of change work is abstracted into a more clearly understood representation although of course the reality is more involved and less 'procedural' looking. It can also be seen how the counsellor bases the change work on the previous understanding and brings it about by the use of just three, well timed and targeted questions.

Level \ Area	Self	Other	Home	Work	Social	System
Overman						
Identity						
Belief						
Values — toward	(H) (F)					
Values — away	?					
Capabilities		1	4			
Experience			(A)	3 ? (E)		
Behaviour — Concepts	(D)			?		
Language	?2	5				
Senses	(C) (G)					
Movement						
Environment						

Figure 17

1. The counsellor asks the client to consider anything at all that might have been enjoyable being with the family at the cinema (A) by asking: 'What is enjoyable, currently, I mean right now, what is enjoyable about being with them? Anything even if it doesn't seems like very much.' Until now the client has thought of being with his family as being either enjoyable or not enjoyable. This means that he has represented his experience in black and white terms. The whole experience has been evaluated as either enjoyable or not. With this question, the counsellor takes the client into the experience to find things from within that were enjoyable so that even if the experience as a whole was not enjoyable, there were aspects that were. This starts to loosen up the previous, more rigid thinking leading to (B) a moving towards value of enjoying the happiness of his children. This feeling is given extra strength when the client is asked to consider the opposite, the children being unhappy.

2. The client is then asked if there is a connection between the warm feeling he gets when seeing the children happy (C) and enjoyment (D) with the question: 'Now, is that feeling, that feeling you get when they are obviously happy, that warm feeling, is that anything like enjoyment?' and he is able to make a connection: 'Well it is yes, I suppose something like enjoyment. It's very easy to take these things for granted.' It's the first time he has considered this but it is a connection that can be built upon.

3. After the client identifies a different feeling at work, like enjoyment but with more buzz he is asked to compare the feeling of buzz and excitement he experiences at work (E) with similar experiences at home with the question: 'And, have you ever felt this way in your home life, at anytime in the past? Even a little bit or something similar.' The client answers: 'Yes, sometimes, if I'm working on a project like fitting the new kitchen or something like that.' At the very least, this places the buzz feeling that had previously only been associated with work into the home context.

4. After exploring this further, the client comes to the conclusion that he could get the same kind of buzz from the challenge of raising the children successfully and this rapidly becomes a new moving towards value (F). 'I think it was when you said challenging, it was like I suddenly felt very strong and determined – you know, like someone has thrown down the gauntlet.'

5. By taking the client through some subjective exercises the counsellor firstly behaviourally links this new motivation with the remembered experience of going to the cinema, allowing the client to relive it differently, now wanting to attend more to his family. In doing this the feeling of challenge changes to a more relaxed feeling of warmth. The counsellor then takes this feeling into the future: 'Now again, keep that feeling very much there in the background and imagine stepping into the future on Thursday night and, even though you don't know precisely all the details, how is it when you imagine how that will be?' This helps to ensure that the new feelings and motivations will successfully transfer into future time with his family.

180

The session finishes with the counsellor inviting the client to reflect a little on what has taken place, helping to safeguard the change work.

As was said earlier, this piece of change work is simply an example of what is possible in therapeutic systemic counselling. It is not presented as a perfect piece and the counsellor could well have taken a different tack altogether. Additionally, the Lifegrid model does not attempt to capture every nuance of the session but rather distil the key components of the problem and the change work. As it turned out, the client attended another five sessions of counselling. More work was done to build his valuing of time spent with his family as well as additional work helping him to learn and develop more effective and efficient cognitive skills to assist the transition from a work context to a home context and vice versa.

By the end of the five sessions, the client was reporting an improved sleep pattern and a noticeable improvement in mood. He had experienced no further panic attacks and was finding spending time with his family enjoyable and fulfilling.

11

Counselling Ethics

Ethics is concerned with how we 'ought' to behave. More specifically it informs and organises how we should conduct ourselves as we go about our day-to-day business, irrespective of what it is we are doing or trying to achieve. Our society is built upon an ethical tradition that we normally acquire as individuals during childhood and for most of the time this almost inherent sense of right and wrong serves us more than adequately. There are certain activities however that requires a little more in the way of ethical guidance and consideration and counselling is one such activity.

Counselling is an activity that creates a special kind of relationship between two people, the counsellor and the client. It is a relationship that often requires quite careful ethical consideration.

Often through, the process of counselling a relationship is formed of quite marked intimacy. Typically, personal issues of a sensitive nature are discussed and explored and this requires a level of intimacy not normally found in a professional relationship. Through this intimate exploration, the client will often expose personal vulnerabilities that an unscrupulous person could easily exploit to his or her own personal gain. The client frequently places the counsellor into the role of 'expert' and this coupled with the fact that the client is often vulnerable and the counselling sessions highly emotionally charged, leads to an imbalance of power. The client becomes more suggestible, placing a large responsibility onto the counsellor to ensure that any guidance given is carefully considered.

Because of this special relationship, counsellors often find themselves embroiled in quite serious ethical dilemmas and have as a profession long recognised the need for ethical guidelines to help steer themselves safely through the potential quagmire of ethical problems. Whilst no guidelines can prepare us for every eventuality, they can at the very least highlight some of the potential issues and prepare us as counsellors with some of the tools necessary for sound ethical resolutions.

Amongst ethical philosophers there is no common agreement on any particular ethical theory. At one extreme, we have those who believe in an absolute ethics. That is, they believe that for any given situation there will always be one and only one ethical course to take and that this will be the case irrespective of variations in context. At the opposite end of the spectrum are the relativists who believe that there is no one right moral code but rather many different moralities relative to the time, culture and context. They believe it is morally wrong to impose one's own ethics onto others.

In the counselling profession, we attempt to be as objective and absolute as possible in creating ethical guidelines, but it has to be recognised that there are times and occasions when the more subjective, relativist way of thinking has to be adopted. No guidelines can ever cover everything or cover every instance or unique set of circumstances. What we need in these situations is a way or method to help ensure we make the best possible choices.

In this chapter, I will attempt to cover most of the major issues faced by the counsellor. I have included a set of ethical guidelines as used by the British Association of Counselling and it is recommended that you familiarise yourself with these. Keep in mind that you may have specific responsibilities to your company or organisation that may conflict with specific guidelines. If this should be the case, be sure to discuss these issues with your manager before making any decisions based on them. Later in the chapter we shall explore some of the ethical issues more specifically related to counselling in the work place.

One of the difficulties with specific guidelines is that there is often disagreement about them. Each of us grows up with our own sense of what is morally right and wrong. Partly this seems to be as a result of acquisition, living in and around ethical people and partly as a result of more deliberate instruction. In our society, the ethical tradition is Christian and mostly our sense of right and wrong is based on the Christian sense of right and wrong, whether we are practicing Christians or not. But, within this, there is considerable room for divergence and there may well be times when you find that the guidelines provided here conflict with your own sense of right and wrong. This is why it is important to fully consider the issues involved and why simply presenting a list of ethical rules doesn't work.

As an example, consider the problems posed by the 'tough love' movement in dealing with drug abuse. Drug abusers will often go to great lengths to feed their habit, thinking nothing of stealing or using those closest to them. About fifteen years ago, several parents of drug abusers got together and realised that ultimately the only way to help their children was to be strong and resist any demands for help from their children. Even if their children were homeless and hungry, if they were abusing drugs, these parents would not help. This approach caused considerable controversy, with many other parents accusing them of being unloving and uncaring. Both sets of parents wanted to help their drug-abusing children but the means they adopted were very different – and how do we decide which approach is ethically correct? As it turned out, many of the detractors of tough love were won over once they had more fully explored the underlying principles with its advocates.

A few years ago, I introduced an exercise to my counselling trainings based on the TV show 'Dilemmas.' In the show, a panel of 'experts' are presented with a scenario where an ethical choice must be made and each is given the opportunity to state what action they would take. However, once they have done this, more information is provided about the scenario that causes them to rethink their choices. This continues for some time with each successive round providing more complex detail than the rounds before until most of the 'experts' are quite tied in knots about what to do. If nothing else, one thing that these exercises have shown me is that we can never be completely sure about the ethical choices we make.

No matter how good a set of guidelines or how thoroughly the issues are explored, there will always remain some doubt and ultimately, in any given situation, we are alone with our ethical decisions.

Another problem sometimes faced by the practicing counsellor is the temptation to impose his or her own ethical values upon the client who might have different sense of right and wrong. This is clearly a problem if the counsellor operates from an absolute ethical code, as at some stage they will come across clients who refuse to follow the same ethical code. Should they try to impose their ethics on the client? Is this itself not an ethical choice? It is certainly easier on the counsellor if he or she operates from a more relativist position where there is tolerance for client differences. The counsellor does need to be both flexible and tolerant of difference if he or she is to avoid such dilemmas.

Whatever guidelines the counsellor uses, I am a firm believer in the idea that prevention is better than cure and for this reason strongly advocate the use of written counsellor/client agreements. This agreement should lay out the scope of counselling expectations and levels of confidentiality the client can expect. Again, although it can not address every eventuality, it will set the tone so that the client is left in no doubt about what to expect, ethically, from their counsellor. At the end of this chapter, you will find a sample agreement contract covering the counselling arrangement between an in-house counsellor accepting referrals from a company personnel department.

In relation to the ethical treatment of the client, there are three central but related issues that need our consideration and these are (a) counsellor competence (b) confidentiality and (c) exploitation. Many other more specific ethical problems stem from these.

Counsellor competence

It is only in the last ten years or so that counselling in this country has become properly recognised as a profession with standards of qualification and professionalism established. Largely this has been down to the work of the British Association of Counselling whose accreditation system is now recognised as the professional standard for practicing counsellors.

But this is only part of the story. For every professionally accredited counsellor practicing in this country there are many, many more utilising counselling skills in their day-to-day work. The qualifications these people possess range from simply being interested in the subject and reading a few books, through to introductory training, basic certification courses, lengthier diploma courses and right up to degree and post-graduate courses.

The question is not so much 'What is the minimum qualification for counselling?' but more, 'What is the appropriate level of counselling for your qualifications and experience?' This is about being aware of the limits of your skills and not taking on counselling problems that are beyond your abilities. For this reason, it is worthwhile having better qualified counselling contacts for you to refer onto.

Deciding this is a very different matter. How can you know, ahead of time, whether you will be able to help somebody with your level of counselling skills? The simple answer is, you can't – which is why at the very basic level of training (which includes the reading of this book and practicing the exercises within) assessment of the counselling needs of a client is so important. At some point in your first session with a client, no matter how informal, you need to spell out that until you know more, it may well be that you'll need to refer the client on to someone more appropriate.

When thinking about counselling competence we need to consider the following:

1. Training and qualifications

There are many levels of training course available for the counselling student. These range from one or two day introductions right through to full degree courses and post-graduate diplomas. Not all training is officially recognised or accredited with organisations such as the BAC, indeed there is nothing to stop anyone from setting up counselling training. When choosing training therefore it is worth spending some time evaluating the credentials of the training organisation.

Other relevant training courses include more specialised courses, seminars and workshops addressing particular problem groups such as alcohol and drug abuse or relationship difficulties and courses in related subjects such as psychology or pharmacology.

2. Experience (general)

Although primarily relating to actual counselling practice, other related work experiences can be relevant to the competence of a counsellor. These might include work in fields such as nursing, teaching or social work where good communication and interpersonal skills are required.

3. Experience (specialised)

Some counsellors chose to specialise in particular areas of counselling, addressing specific problems such as drug and alcohol abuse or working with particular client groups such as retirement, redundancy or bereavement. It goes without saying that a specialised counsellor would in general be more appropriate for clients experiencing the problem they are specialised in than a more generic counsellor, even if that counsellor were to have more overall experience.

4. Availability

No matter how competent a counsellor in terms of qualifications or experience, if they have not got the required time available for a specific client then they are not appropriate for that client's needs. There is a general standard in counselling that clients should be seen for one hour once a week but there are clients who may require much more than this, just as there are clients who require less. Assessing the frequency and duration of counselling for any given client is an important aspect of a counsellor's general competence.

The following criteria can be used as a general guide to the level of competence required. These are based loosely on the BAC requirements and/or the United Kingdom Psychotherapy Council requirements.

Level of Problem	Competence
Supportive Counselling	• Reading a few books on counselling through to one to five day introductory courses • Regular counselling practice of at least one hour per week • Supervision with a more experienced counsellor.
Problem Solving Counselling	• Certificate level qualification in counselling • Regular counselling practice of at least five hours per week. • Supervision with a more experienced counsellor.
Therapeutic Counselling	• Diploma level qualification in counselling or Psychotherapy • Regular counselling practice of at least five hours per week • At least one year's experience of supportive and problem solving counselling • Supervision with a more experienced counsellor or psychotherapist • In addition it is recommended that a counsellor practicing therapeutic counselling should have a good grasp of general psychology topics including human development, communication, cognitive functioning and behavioural psychology.

The counsellor has a responsibility to ensure that he or she is practicing at an appropriate level of competence and taking on clients that he or she is not competent to handle is considered extremely unprofessional practice.

In many professions, it is now considered necessary to continually update skill levels and understanding though regular training and counselling is no different. This is especially so if there is a long gap between periods of counselling practice. If you are practicing supportive counselling on a fairly limited basis, then it is possibly enough to refresh your understanding with some reading on the subject every now and again but it is recommended that you attend some kind of related training, seminar or conference from time to time. If you are practicing problem solving or therapeutic counselling then in addition to attending conferences or seminars you should update your training as required by any professional body you belong to or, failing that, you should ensure that you attend more specialist counselling training at least once a year. It is recommended that you also join a practice or peer supervision group.

Although supervision is considered a part of the counsellor's overall competence because it is an important aspect in its own right, it is addressed as a separate topic later in this chapter.

Confidentiality

Because of the sometimes sensitive and personal nature of counselling, it is not surprising that the details of a counselling session should be treated as confidential by the counsellor and most counsellors strive to ensure high levels of confidentiality. Without this, it is unlikely that clients would feel free and able to share their thoughts and concerns. In this, counselling is no different from many other professions such as law and medicine. However, like many aspects of counselling ethics, the maintenance of confidentiality is a tricky and delicate responsibility. More problematically within the profession of counselling, there is no overall agreement on the scope of confidentiality.

Some organisations, such as The Samaritans, and some individual counsellors, advocate a policy of complete and utter confidentiality.

They feel that unless they can guarantee this, clients will never feel completely sure that they can open up and discuss their problems satisfactorily. This is a highly contentious issue. Take, for example sex offenders. Whilst many consider them criminals who need nothing more than appropriate punishment, there are many who work with sex offenders trying to rehabilitate them. What happens when a sex offender client opens up to the counsellor about offences that have not been reported before? How confidential should this information be? What are the responsibilities of the counsellor in these circumstances? Should the counsellor report the offences to the police and violate confidentiality or should he or she maintain confidentiality in order to work more effectively with the client? There are no easy answers to any of these questions but they do highlight some of the difficulties with client confidentiality.

In many professions, a more moderate version of client confidentiality is now practiced whereby limits are placed on what can remain confidential and what can't and although this helps, it does not completely overcome the inherent problems of client confidentiality. It is however, highly recommended that you should take this approach in any counselling work you undertake. More specifically a boundary needs to be established from the outset that states clearly what kind of information would fall beyond the limits of confidentiality. The client is then left with a choice, they either continue counselling knowing that there are limits in place or they seek help elsewhere.

Many counsellors take the relatively easy option of establishing the scope of confidentiality as including any issue that does not break the law. Beyond the scope of confidentiality is any information that pertains to criminal activity that has either been committed or which will be committed. The client is informed of this from the outset of counselling and if at any time the counsellor feels that the client is about to reveal something beyond the scope of confidentiality, he or she should be warned again that the counsellor may not be able to keep in confidence, what is about to be revealed.

It may be, that because of your own personal convictions or beliefs, you wish to place other issues beyond the limits of confidentiality and this is fine as long as the limits are made clear to the client. What is not fine is if confidentiality is broken without prior warning to the client.

As well as confidentiality of information shared during counselling, there is also the issue of confidentiality that the client is receiving counselling. Under no circumstances should the counsellor reveal to a third party that a particular client is receiving counselling unless this has been previously agreed with the client or unless the client has divulged information that lies beyond the limits of what can remain confidential. In other words, if a client reveals information regarding criminal activity and it has previously been agreed that such information lies beyond the limits of confidentiality, then the counsellor would be ethically entitled to reveal the identity of the client to the Police although it may be possible to not reveal the nature of the counsellor's relationship with the client.

Beyond this, there are other issues that the practicing counsellor needs to consider. Specifically when the counsellor is practicing in the workplace.

If the counsellor is practicing in the workplace but is not employed in any other capacity by the company or organisation they are counselling for, then there are issues concerned with who the client actually is. Is the client the person who receives counselling or is the client the company or organisation who employs and pays the counsellor? The answer is that they are both clients and as such great care needs to be taken to establish the limits of confidentiality. Exactly what information can and can't be passed on to the employer should be spelled out very carefully so that no one is left with any doubt. The counsellor should strive to keep such information to a minimum in order to guarantee greater confidentiality. On the other hand, the company or organisation will in all likelihood want more information than the counsellor is likely to want to give. They are paying the bill after all. This needs to be negotiated and it is worthwhile having a written contract with the company or organisation detailing the limits of client confidentiality. Even then, the counsellor should keep information passed on to the company or organisation to a useful minimum. The main priority and responsibility for the counsellor is the client sat before them and their responsibility to the client should always take precedence over their responsibility to the company or organisation

Exploitation

Because there is an imbalance of power within the counselling relationship, with the client often placing himself or herself in a seemingly vulnerable position, great care should be taken to avoid exploitation of the client.

It should I hope, go without saying that the counsellor should never knowingly exploit the client's vulnerable position for personal gain but, it is still worth spelling out some of the ways this might happen. Even the best counsellors are capable of self-deception.

Financial exploitation

The most obvious way that a counsellor might exploit a client is financially. If your remit is confined to the workplace, counselling fellow employees as part of your job, then it is unlikely that the financing of counselling will ever be an issue. But, if you do find yourself in the position of having to charge for your counselling services, it is important that the full implications of this are spelled out to the client.

Counselling, unlike many other professions, is not an exact science with easily measurable results, therefore payment by results is not a realistic option. The counsellor should always make this clear from the outset. Never promise a specific outcome. This has to be balanced with client confidence in the counsellor and it is therefore acceptable to reassure the client that you as a counsellor feel confident that you can help in some way.

Wherever possible, try to make clear, ahead of time, what the likely financial cost will be. Many counsellors offer the first assessment session free of charge and part of that assessment is the likely duration and full cost of counselling. The client is then able to make an informed choice.

Sexual exploitation

Under no circumstances should a counsellor partake in sexual activity with a client whilst that client is receiving counselling. Irrespective of other moral considerations, it is not at all uncommon for clients to develop a 'crush' on their counsellor thus rendering them vulnerable to sexual exploitation.

It must however be understood that typically counselling involves two adults generally accepted as being responsible for their own choices. If either the client or counsellor therefore feel that they have genuine feelings of attraction or love for the other, then counselling should terminate immediately. In some, occasional situations, it may be ethically acceptable for the counsellor and client to develop a more intimate relationship but only after a suitable cooling off period following the termination of counselling. At least three months is the generally accepted period. This only really applies to supportive and problem-solving counselling. In the case of therapeutic counselling and especially in the situation where the issues being explored are of a sexual nature, it is unacceptable for the counsellor to engage in any sexual activity with the client at any time during or following counselling.

Personal betterment

Because of the sometimes sensitive nature of counselling, there may be times when the counsellor could exploit what they have learned to better either their own or some third party's personal or work situation. This is more likely to be so if both the counsellor and client are working for the same employer. Needless to say, this should not happen under any circumstances and, when counselling in the workplace, the counsellor needs to take specific safeguards to prevent this.

Firstly, the counsellor needs to take a look at the professional relationships shared by him/herself and the client. Do they or might they in the future share the same manager? Do they or might they report to someone who has an influence on the client's working life? If yes to either of these, the counsellor may need to consider whether he or she is the appropriate person to counsel. This should in any case, always be discussed with the client and counselling should only proceed with the full and informed consent of the client.

Secondly, the counsellor needs to consider whether he or she may at any time in the future be in direct competition with the client for career development or promotion. If this could be the case, then counselling should not proceed.

Lastly, the counsellor needs to consider whether anyone he or she is involved with on a personal level might benefit from knowing details about the client and take safeguards to ensure that confidence can be maintained.

Self-aggrandisement

It is considered ethically wrong and an exploitation of the client if the sole motivation for counselling is self-aggrandisement. That is not to say that a counsellor shouldn't take pride in his or her work and satisfaction from a job well done, but the primary purpose and motivation for any counselling should be to assist the client, not to assist the counsellor.

Whilst this is not usually an issue, there are times when it can become one, most notably if the counselling proves unsuccessful and the client doesn't feel helped. At such times, it is vitally important that no blame be placed at the feet of the client for the failure of the client. Historically, some clients have been described as 'resistive' when counselling fails. This is bad practice and clients should never be given such labels. The counsellor should be perfectly happy and prepared to admit when they have been unable to help and suggest other ways in which the client might be helped.

There is one additional, common ethical problem faced by the counsellor in the workplace and that concerns the degree of autonomy the client has. In private practice, counsellors usually take referrals from the client themselves or from fellow professionals. In either case, the client attends counselling on a purely voluntary basis. In the workplace however we can not always be quite so certain that clients are attaining counselling because they want help or because they are attending counselling when a manger has requested it in an attempt to solve some problem he or she is having with the client. There needn't be anything sinister about this – many managers send their employees to counselling for genuine reasons and it may well be that the client would benefit enormously from counselling. But the fact remains that unless clients are in counselling of their own choosing, helping them is difficult if not impossible. Counselling is an activity that requires the full and total commitment of the client. Clients who have been ordered or coerced into counselling are, in our experience, unlikely to show that kind of commitment. At best, they will play along to keep the boss happy, at worst, they will be angry and resentful. Ensure that all clients, whether you are counselling them formally or simply using counselling skills in your day-to-day work to help them, are engaging freely and of their own will.

As well as these specific ethical responsibilities to clients, counsellors have other responsibilities both to themselves and, in the case of counselling in the workplace, their employers.

Supervision

Counselling supervision is not the same as the hierarchical supervision most of us are used to in our place of work and the two should never be confused. Specifically, counselling supervision is the supervision of the counsellor by another competent counsellor who has no other direct or indirect professional relationship with the counsellor, i.e. they have no line management responsibilities. The reason for this is that counsellors should feel safe to divulge concerns about their own counselling shortcomings and that they might therefore feel compromised in this if the supervisor is someone whom they also report to as a line manager.

Anyone who engages in any form of counselling activity should receive appropriate professional supervision. This not only safeguards the clients, it also helps safeguard the counsellors in helping to monitor their counselling activities. How much supervision is required is another matter. As a rough guide, a full-time counsellor should receive at least two hours supervision a month. The less counselling performed, the less supervision is required but, it is ultimately the counsellors' responsibility to ensure that they are receiving adequate supervision and irrespective of any normal supervision arrangements counsellors should always seek supervision if they are struggling with any aspect of their counselling work.

Above and beyond this, if you are practicing counselling in the workplace, your employers may have their own standards for supervision and the counsellor should seek advice on this before the commencement of any counselling activity.

Record keeping

The keeping of records is a controversial issue, with many counsellors arguing that as long as records exist they cannot fully guarantee their clients' confidentiality. For this reason, there is no real agreement on whether records should or shouldn't be kept. However, with cases of litigation on the increase, it can also be argued that record keeping is of vital importance to counsellors in protecting themselves from possible legal action.

If records are kept, it is important to consider the following:

1. Does the client agree to the keeping of records and to the nature of the information contained within these records?
2. Is there agreement with the client to allow unlimited access to any records kept?
3. Who else might have access to these records and is the client aware of any third parties who may have access?
4. Who legally owns any records kept? If you are practicing counselling in the workplace as an employee, this is not a straightforward issue and the organisation you work for may claim that they have ownership. Before keeping any records on clients, clarify the situation on this with your employer.
5. If counselling at work, are you required to report to the referrer in either verbal or written form and if so, is there agreement on the exact nature of these reports and is the client in agreement with them.

As long as all of the above are checked and clients are fully aware of what the situation is regarding their records, then it is strongly advised that records be kept. At the very least, these should include the date and time of any counselling sessions and any specific concerns the counsellor may have.

Insurance

If counselling as a private individual, then it is important that the counsellor has at the very least professional liability insurance to cover against possible legal action taken against him or her by clients. Most professional organisations such as the BAC and UKCP will only accept as members practitioners who are covered by insurance and most will provide contact details of insurance companies specialising in this field.

If you are counselling in the workplace, then your company's insurance policies should cover you but it is as well to check on this before engaging in any counselling activity.

Ultimately, it is rare to find precise answers to ethical problems but these guidelines should at least prepare you for the kinds of issues you are likely to encounter. If you really do find that you're in an ethical dilemma that you can see no way out of, then it is time for you to discuss the issue with your supervisor (another good reason for supervision). He or she won't be able to answer the problem for you but in these types of situations, two heads are definitely better than one.

Finally in this chapter, I have included a link to an excellent set of ethical guidelines that can be found at the BACP website. This is their Ethical Framework for Good Practice in Counselling and Psychotherapy, which can be found at:

http://www.bacp.co.uk/members_visitors/public_information/pu blic_frameset5.htm.

Glossary

Abstraction   The process of creating more general meaning from sensory specific experience. Language is one of the main tools of abstraction. Alfred Kozybski's *General Semantics* explores the process of abstraction in great depth.

Adaptation   Within any given system, components of that system may require to change in some way in response to changes to other aspects of that system. Adaptation is the process whereby creatures evolve in response to environmental changes. Humans are highly adaptable.

Affective   Anything concerned with affect or human emotion. In systemic counselling, we often talk about 'affective change', a change in a person's emotional state, as different from 'effective change', a change in cognition or behaviour.

Analogue   We describe gradual and non-discrete change as analogue. Like the hands of a watch, the change is continuous as opposed to the digital watch that makes discrete jumps as it changes. A distinction is therefore made between analogue processes and digital processes. We often think of visual representations as analogue in nature as opposed to language which is clearly digital.

Anxiety   A heightened state of physiological and mental activity that accompanies fear. Anxiety often results from anticipated problems or difficulties. In extreme cases anxiety can develop into a runaway pattern which results in what is often referred to as a 'Panic Attack'. During a panic attack, the sufferer's level of arousal goes far beyond what is required, rendering them quite dysfunctional.

Attitude

A cognitive and psychological complex in relation to some activity or situation, attitude helps determine how we will relate to and behave towards changes in our ongoing situation. Attitudes can be thought of as more or les useful.

Beliefs

Cognitive structures that we build through experience and use to help organise our behaviour and functioning. Beliefs are concerned with how we think or expect ourselves and the world to behave, what we think is required and what we think is possible. Most beliefs are concerned with the mundane of everyday life In systemic counselling, we often make the distinction between useful and less useful beliefs and not between true and false beliefs.

Bottom Up

Any process that begins from the lower level of much detail and works its way up to a higher level. The process of abstraction is often thought of as a bottom up process.

Calibration

A complex process taken from the field of cybernetics. When we calibrate, we establish a means by which we can measure some phenomenon or process we are engaged in. If we wished to measure the length of a piece of wood, we would first need to establish meaningful units of measurement by setting our measuring device to some already know measurement. Humans often instinctively calibrate to such things as danger and reward.

Client-centered   The distinction is made between approaches to counselling that focus primarily on the problem and those that focus primarily on the person as a whole. The former is known as problem-centered, the latter as client-centered. Most forms of counselling utilise a client-centered approach as this is generally considered to be of more lasting benefit.

Closed questions   A closed question is a question that requires only a yes or no answer such as 'Are you feeling better?' Closed questions are not considered useful in many counselling situations as they do not help establish more divergent, exploratory processing on the part of the client.

Cognitive   Behaviours and processes of thought including the processes of abstraction and the building of meaning, relating, reasoning and concluding.

Congruence   When all parts of a system are in harmony, they are considered to be congruent with one another. A person who is in two minds about some decision is considered incongruent in that there is an internal disagreement or disharmony. In counselling we often describe communications in terms of the degree of congruence. If a person fully convinces us of what he or she is saying, then we might describe their communication as congruent.

Conscious   That which we are aware of at any given time. Some cognitive processes such as logical reasoning, reflecting and decision making are often considered conscious processes in that we are aware that we are doing them. However, we are mostly unaware of precisely how we carry out these processes. This aspect of our cognition is largely unconscious. The distinctions between conscious and unconscious is not a fixed one and at any one time we will be more or less aware (conscious) of differing aspects of our ongoing experience. Consequently much will be unconscious or taking place beyond our awareness. Unconscious processes can be made conscious in that they can be brought into our awareness and vice versa.

Constructivist   A branch of philosophical psychology that proposes that our sense of the world or the meaning that we create is actively constructed through processes of abstraction and not just passively received. To the constructivist, there can be no absolute knowledge or sense of absolute reality – there is only ever our subjective view point although we can strive for greater objectivity.

Convergent   Any process that brings two or more processes or things closer together. Coming to a conclusion can be thought of as a convergent process in that, as options are eliminated, there is a coming together or unification of intent.

Cybernetics   The study of information flow and control in complex systems including machines and man. Cybernetics came into being during the 1930s and 40s with the advent of more complex machines such as computers. Older models of energy and energy flow were no longer adequate in explaining the complexities of these machines. Soon it was realised that these same principles could be applied to human systems and communication in man.

Developmental Behavioural Modelling (DBM)   Developed from NLP, DBM is an ever-burgeoning science of human processing and change. A constructivist approach that considers not just what we experience but also how and why we experience and behave in the way we do. Unlike traditional psychology DBM is not so concerned with the absolute truths of psychological theory but more with the behavioural skills of useful modelling as a tool to understanding. The application of DBM to psychotherapy and counselling resulted in Systemic Counselling.

Depression   A state of mind often resulting from a reaction to life events where cognitive processes become dulled. The depressed person often feels sad and tearful and unable to cope with the simplest of tasks.

Digital   See analogue.

Divergent   The opposite of convergent. In divergent processes, there is a spreading out of new processes or things. Divergent thinking is often used during periods of exploration when all the options need to be considered. Brainstorming is a good example of a divergent process.

Ecological   An ecology is any large complex system with interdependent parts. Changes to any one part of such a system may be described as ecological if they negatively affect the system as a whole. The term is often used in talking about the condition of our earth and in particular the condition of the natural world but this is only one example. Human change can be both ecological and unecological. As counsellors we strive to help bring about ecological change.

Effective   See affective.

202

Empathy   The ability to put ourselves 'into the shoes' of others, to see and understand the world from their point of view. The ability to empathise with the client is considered important in many client-centered forms of counselling.

Feedback   A technical term used in cybernetics to describe the type of information received by a system. Feedback can either be negative, where there is news of a difference, or positive where there is no news of a difference. All information is necessarily negative feedback. In human terms, we can think of negative feedback as being any sensed news of a difference. Positive feedback is no sensed news of a difference. When we are receiving positive feedback, there is no need for us to alter our current behaviour. Negative feedback provides with the opportunity to change or adapt our behaviour.

Flashback   A psychological phenomenon that often follows from some traumatic event whereby the sufferer experiences a vivid reliving of the event. Flashbacks occur beyond the conscious control of the sufferer and are often of such intensity that the sufferer is re-traumatised by the flashback.

Fractal   Patterns that recur in a similar fashion at all levels of magnification. In systemic counselling, the language model has a fractal structure.

Frames   Frames are psychological structures that help provide meaning to experience. Examples include learning frame and performance frame. The same events will have a different meaning and impact if they are experienced within a larger learning frame than if in a larger performance frame. Reframing is a well known NLP technique for changing the meaning of experience.

General Semantics Developed early in the 20th Century by Alfred Korzybski. The study of the process of abstraction and therefore meaning.

Gestalt Therapy A form of psychotherapy popularised by Fritz Perls in the 1950s and 60s where the main focus is on the clients' feelings and their development from past unresolved issues. Gestalt therapy advocates the expression of negative emotions.

Holistic Holistic approaches to counselling and health care consider the whole person, mind-body-environment to be of importance and not just the single components.

Intuition Intuition is often thought of as an instinctive ability to know something without having perceived it, or a sixth sense. NLP shows us that what we normally think of as intuition is probably just the result of highly tuned sensory acuity operating at a largely unconscious level.

Kinaesthetic Used in NLP to encompass all that is described as 'feeling'. This includes the feelings of touch as well as more abstract, emotional feelings such as anger or joy.

Leading Term used to describe the behavioural influence of one person over another whilst in high levels of rapport.

Linear A linear process is one which proceeds in one direction where one event or phenomenon follows from another. Linear processes are common in the inanimate world of matter where cause and effect relationships can be found, but in the world of the animate or living, processes are often more circular and nested, i.e. feedback and calibration loops in information processing.

Matching   In NLP, behavioural matching of behaviours is taught as a technique for establish and developing rapport. Matching or 'pacing' is often the precursor to leading (see above)

Mind   A product of the nervous system or perhaps any sufficiently complex system of information exchange. Mind encompasses all conscious and many unconscious processes of thought and feeling. In systemic counselling, mind and body are considered different aspects or different levels of description of the one whole and not as two distinct entities.

Model   Any simplified representation of a phenomenon. Models can be more or less complex and more or less useful. In contrast to theories which are attempts to show how the world 'really is' and therefore concerned with truth, models are usually evaluated on how useful they are where truth is less important.

Modelling   The process of building a model. In psychological terms, modelling is another way of describing the process by which we build our understanding of the world. We represent the world through various cognitive structures in a simplified way.

Nested   Where one process or thing exists within another. We often

Neuro-Linguistic Programming   The study of the structure of human experience. Established in the 1970s, NLP has produced many useful models of communication and change and has a big influence on the development and practice of Systemic Counselling.

Non-Verbal   Behaviours that are communications but not linguistic. All communication contains both verbal and non-verbal aspects and both are considered important. Non-verbal communication includes such things as voice tone, facial expression and gesticulation.

Objective   Facts or knowledge that is free from any bias or other subjective influences. Objective knowledge of the world is the goal of science, to bring about knowledge that is externally verifiable. A constructivist philosophy argues that objective knowledge is impossible in that subjectivity necessarily influences our understanding. The best we can hope for is to become more objective in our understanding.

Open questions   An open question is one that can not be answered with either yes or no. Open questions require lengthier answers and are useful for encouraging a person to explain in more depth or to explore their own thoughts. A question such as 'How do you feel?' is a good example of an open question and can be distinguished from the similar but closed question. 'Are you feeling okay?'

Personal space   The space around us that we experience as belonging to us. Usually about one arm's length away, we can quickly become uncomfortable if others come into this space. As a rule we prefer to keep strangers at 'arms length' or outside our personal space. In Systemic Counselling, personal space is used as a construct for helping develop rapport.

Psychiatry   A branch of medicine concerned with the treatment of disorders of the mind most typically using medication and/or other medical approaches to illness.

Psychology   The science and study of the mind.

Psychotherapy   A non-medical approach to helping people suffering
                        from emotional or psychological difficulties.
                        Psychotherapy comes in many different forms and
                        differs from psychiatry in that the psychotherapist is
                        not so concerned with a diagnostic model.
                        Psychotherapy normally takes the form of a one-on-
                        one interaction but group psychotherapy is also
                        popular.

Rapport   A measure of the quality of relating between two or
                        more people. The greater the mutual influence, the
                        greater the rapport. Rapport can often be externally
                        verified by the degree to which those concerned are
                        matching and pacing each other's behaviour.

Remodelling   An approach to change used in Systemic Counselling
                        where the counsellor helps change the client's model
                        of understanding. At a more advanced level, the
                        counsellor may not only remodel the client's model of
                        the world but also remodel the very way he or she
                        builds their models.

Representational   Our five representational systems are based on the
Systems   five senses and are the modes by which we represent
                        information subjectively. For example, we can think
                        using pictures, sounds or feelings.

Self-esteem   A measure of how good we feel about ourselves.

Sensory acuity   A measure of the sensitivity of our sensing of the
                        world.

States   Often used in NLP as a catch-all description of any
                        given internal state of mind/body.

Strategies   An NLP term to describe learned and repeatable skills, often cognitive in nature. For example, we may use a strategy for decision making that remains essentially the same in structure and process irrespective of any given content.

Stress   Initially a specialised physiological response to any perceived danger or threat. Prolonged exposure to the perceived threat can lead to a state of chronic stress and breakdown.

Subjective   Our internal experience of the world. Constructivist philosophy argues that we can never escape our subjectivity, that we must always necessarily perceive the world through the blinkers and bias of our subjectivity.

Submodalities   The various ways in which we represent the world. For example, if we have a subjective picture of some memory, that picture will among other things have a certain intensity, brightness and clarity to it. These 'submodalities' are variably differing from one experience to another and help organise and determine how we react to our own representations.

Sympathy   Feeling sorrow or pity for the plight or pain of another without necessarily feeling their pain. One step removed from empathy, sympathy is not generally considered a particular useful attitude in counselling.

Systemic   Concerning a whole system of inter-relating parts. In Systemic Counselling for example, the client is never seen as an isolated individual but rather as a part of other, larger human systems.

Top-down   The organising of lower level detail by higher level structures. For example, it is now widely recognised that the way we perceive the world is directly influenced by the beliefs we have about the world. Our senses are influenced 'top-down' by our beliefs.

Unconscious   Any subjective process that occurs outside our awareness is considered unconscious. We are unconscious of many of the ways in which we think and reason, even when we are conscious of the results of such thoughts.

Validation   In counselling, a form of reassurance where the client's experience, no matter how unacceptable to the client, is recognised and acknowledged by the counsellor. Through time, the client comes to feel accepted as a whole person, warts and all.

Values   Psychological structures that help determine how we seek out experience. Values can be thought of as both our orientations towards those things we desire and away from those things we find unpleasant. .

Contacts

David McNorton's contact details can be found at his website:

www.davidmcnorton.co.uk

davidmcnorton@ntlworld.com

For full diploma training in Systemic Counselling and details of other training events, contact:

Sensory Systems Training Ltd
162 Queens Drive, Queens Park
Glasgow, G42 8QN
tel: 0141 424 4177

www.sensorysystems.co.uk

info@sensorysystems.co.uk

Other useful contacts:

The British Association of Counselling and Psychotherapy
BACP House, 35-37 Albert Street
Rugby, Warwickshire, CV21 2SG
tel: 0870 4435252

www.bacp.co.uk

United Kingdom Council for Psychotherapy
167-169 Great Portland Street
London, W1W 5PF
tel: 020 7436 3002

www.ukcp.org.uk

ukcp@psychotherapy.org.uk

Index